SIP

SIPSMITH®
London

ABOUT THE AUTHOR:

Master Distiller of Sipsmith. Drinks historian. Underwear model. Book publisher. Bon viveur. Cotswold gardener. Gin lover. Creative genius. Jared poured his heart and soul (and plenty of gin) into this book, for which we are forever grateful.

An Hachette UK Company
www.hachette.co.uk

First published in Great Britain in 2019 by Mitchell Beazley,
an imprint of Octopus Publishing Group Ltd
Carmelite House
50 Victoria Embankment
London EC4Y 0DZ
www.octopusbooks.co.uk

ISBN 978-1-78472-608-9

A CIP catalogue record for this book is available from the British Library.

Printed and bound in China

3 5 7 9 10 8 6 4

All drinks serve one unless otherwise stated.

Commissioning Editor: Joe Cottington
Editor: Ella Parsons
Copy Editor: Emily Preece-Morrison
Art Director: Yasia Williams-Leedham
Photographer: Yuki Sugiura
Mixologist: Missy Flynn
Stylist: Lucy Attwater
Cover Illustrator: Maggie Enterrios
Senior Production Controller: Allison Gonsalves

SIP

100
Gin Cocktails
with only 3 ingredients

by the Founders of

SIPSMITH®
London

(Mainly Jared, to be honest)

MITCHELL BEAZLEY

CONTENTS

'Perfection is achieved, not when there is nothing more to add, but when there is nothing left to take away.'

Antoine de Saint-Exupéry

INTRODUCTION

Beauty in simplicity

Stunning doesn't have to be complicated. Certainly, there are amazing cocktails made by amazing bartenders the world over, with myriad ingredients, complicated quasi-scientific equipment and years of dedication to the art of mixology. Should us mere mortals attempt one of these fat-washed, oak-smoked drinks at home, we are likely to feel intimidated by the task and default back to one of our staples. It is easy to reach for a glass of wine or a gin and tonic. Neither are bad options, but what a shame if the wonderful world of diverse gin enjoyments is so close yet remains out of grasp.

It is said that once a cocktail recipe has more than three ingredients, more than nine out of ten of us lose the inclination to continue and elect to make or have something simpler. The good news is that hidden among the thousands of recipes out there are hundreds of truly delicious gin cocktails with no more than three ingredients – drinks that are easy and quick to make.

The fact that they are straightforward isn't a negative; it is their strength. Indeed, many of these simple three-ingredient combinations are the foundations for more complicated recipes. With fewer ingredients, you can get to the core of those great ingredients as well.

In many ways this has parallels with our own story at Sipsmith. We didn't set out to make the most complicated gin recipe in the world. Neither did we look to use ingredients that no one in the long, illustrious (and sometimes contentious) history of gin had considered. That wasn't the point. Quite the reverse. Sipsmith Gin was born out of a desire to remember where and how gin began and when it reached its crescendo of handcrafted quality – to recapture that essence of the quintessential London Dry Gin, made the way it used to be made, the way it should be made.

We looked at the classic gin recipes from the 18th and 19th centuries. We used ingredients that wouldn't have been a surprise to the distillers of old. The skill was in finding the right balance between those simple ingredients to deliver the classic London Dry Gin style.

Taking shortcuts is crafty. Doing things properly – that's craft.

In the spirit of finding that beauty in simplicity, we avoided shortcuts. When we started in 2009, the received wisdom in the industry was that the sensible way was to make gin concentrate. That means you take a much larger quantity of gin botanicals than you need for distillation, load them into the still, collect the concentrated gin distillate and then dilute it with neutral alcohol to end up with gin. This is so common that it is in the legal definition of London Dry Gin: nothing can be added after distillation except neutral spirit and water. There is no limit to the quantity of spirit, so the minimum amount of pot stilling is done and a maximum of neutral spirit is added afterwards. It makes money, but to us it made

no sense. We wanted to go back to the old-school traditional methodology of 'one-shot distillation', where a distiller would only use the right amount of ingredients for one batch. The distillate that is collected: that's the gin. Keep it simple – no adulteration, no added spirit after distillation, simply the art of the distiller to load the still, make the cuts and get the recipe right in one shot.

By adopting this philosophy, rejecting the shortcuts and doing it the right way, Sipsmith unwittingly kicked off the craft gin revival. Right back in London, where the history of gin started a few hundred years ago, it began again.

If there was one principal criticism levelled at us at the time (other than the extremely prosaic failure to optimise operational efficiency), it was that it would be almost impossible to achieve perfect consistency from batch to batch. The concentrate method dumbs down the character of any individual distillation run,

by dint of dilution, whereas our inherited one-shot method leaves this character out there for all to taste. It isn't easy to make a decision to zag when everyone else is zigging, but that is precisely what we did. It was Fairfax's father, a silversmith, who reassured us that the world valued complexity and character in the realm of the artisan. Perfect consistency is the preserve of the machine, of the infinitely replicable production-line process, designed beyond everything to drive down cost. Smithery is the art of the craftsman. It is the process by which something that has a certain intrinsic value is crafted, through skill, love and dedication, into something considerably more valuable. It is special precisely because it is a reflection of the craftsman who made it and the character that it takes on as a result.

Inconsistency between batches, pah! We know that we want people to enjoy essentially the same taste profile from batch to batch. Let's be clear; this is not the same as making wine, where there are great, average and poor vintages. Every bottle of Sipsmith Gin is a bottle that we are delighted with. But they do have character. There are subtle differences. There must be, as they are the reflection of a personal balance of science and art in the hands of the distiller who made them.

To remind ourselves of this, we took on the moniker '-smith'. We just needed the right prefix. Sipping has the perfect connotation of lingering over and treasuring something truly special. So, Sipsmith it is. Just as wordsmiths love all things wordical, we love all things sippical – and we especially love gin.

The power of three

Heads, hearts and tails. These three elements describe the distillation process. It is a well-documented cultural phenomenon that we like things in threes. From the religious – the Holy Trinity, the Three Wise Men, the three realms of earth, heaven and hell – to the secular and the role of three in our folklore, mythology and literature, three is powerfully interwoven into the fabric of our society and has a special significance for us all. Sigmund Freud has explored it extensively. Shakespeare used it in many of his works. From the power of those three little words that mean so much to say and to hear (and they're not Drink More Gin), to the very nature of the way that we construct history: beginning, middle, end; past, present, future... Is it a coincidence that three of us started Sipsmith and this book is all about the beauty of just three ingredients? Of course not.

With the right gin, if you really pare it right back, you only need three ingredients for a perfect drink: gin, ice and a glass; plus a couple of great friends to sip it with.

Happy sipping!

Sam, Fairfax and Jared

A VERY BRIEF HISTORY OF GIN

Facts to impress fellow sippers

Sipsmith have proudly played a key part in gin's modern history, primarily by reaching back into the depths of gin's history. So, we thought this was a great opportunity to rewrite it and set a few records straight. And the gin resurgence that kicked off in 2009? We know a little bit about who started that, too. Read on – or skip straight down to the bottom – for that part.

The story of gin is the story of juniper. Juniper is the flavour that transforms distilled spirit into gin. As with most distillates, its roots are medicinal. It traces back to early alchemists searching for the 'water of life'. Juniper has a colourful place in medical history quite apart from its role in alcohol.

When the Black Death swept across Europe, between 1347 and 1353, it was thought to be spread by bad odours. Juniper in particular was supposed to ward off those noxious fumes. It seems that medieval folks were unaware that juniper oil is a reasonably effective flea repellent – and it was fleas that carried the plague.

In the post-plague years, juniper remained a favoured flavour for the European palate. In Holland, genever – a medicinal spirit in which juniper was infused into alcohol – emerged during the 16th century. By the early 1600s, English distillers produced a spirit with a formula surprisingly similar to modern-day gin: one that included juniper, orange and lemon peels and spices. Most of this alcohol was relegated to apothecaries, where it was prescribed to patients for a variety of ailments. Back then, it probably wasn't the most pleasant medicine.

By the time England saw King William III of Orange and his co-monarch and wife Mary ascend to the throne in 1688, the country was on course for the 'Gin Craze'. Waging war with France, the monarchs saw an easy way to curtail importation of French spirits and wine by encouraging domestic grain production and the distillation of spirits from that bounty. Practically overnight, Parliament levelled new taxes and licensing on beer and ale, causing brewed beverages to skyrocket in price and distilled spirits to become a cheap alternative. In 1714,

Parliament stated that London needed more distilleries and smoothed the way to make that possible. By 1721, in some areas of London there was a working gin still in one out of four habitable structures. Records indicate that two million gallons of gin were produced that year alone.

It wasn't until 1728 that Parliament realised that unregulated distilling caused citizens harm all across the nation. And it wasn't until 1736 that the government took action against the unbridled distillation and compounding of spirits, coming up with the first marginally-effective legislation the following year. Periodically, further Acts popped up over the following decades, culminating in the Act of 1823, which made it nearly impossible to appeal a rejection if you applied for a distiller's licence and your still capacity was smaller than 1,800 litres. It was this Act we had to render toothless so that Sipsmith could begin distilling in London.

After a period of inevitable decline as a result of these rigorous rules, modern gin history begins. There were twelve distilleries making gin in Britain when, in December 2008, Sipsmith received the first new license in London in nearly two hundred years. It took over two years of legal work to get that license, legal work that kicked open the doors for a deluge of other small start-ups – 486 of them at the time of writing. Sipsmith led the charge, launching a boom that has reverberated around the world.

However, in 2009, Sipsmith was just three guys in a tiny London garage with one still. 'Export' was anywhere outside London. 'Distribution' was Sam's moped. And it seemed that few people under 60 wanted to talk about – much less drink – gin.

Sipsmith's goal was to reach back to the 1860s, when distilling technology was producing flawless base spirit but the rectification process had not yet been widely industrialised. Gin was made in one shot on copper pot stills. We reached back to how gin used to be made, how it should be made. And we hoped that someone out there would share our passion. It felt like a tight underground community at first, a secret society of unabashed gin lovers. But something this good couldn't remain a secret forever.

WHERE THE MAGIC HAPPENS

How gin is made

To make gin, you begin with neutral spirit – pure ethyl alcohol. And you need juniper.

Place these into a copper pot still with enough distilled water to cut the spirit to about 60 per cent alcohol. It must contain juniper to be gin. (In fact, this is where the word gin comes from; it is a shortening of the French word for juniper, *genièvre*.)

You can add other botanicals to accentuate the flavour of the juniper, as nearly all distillers do. There are dozens of common gin botanicals, but the most standard ones are dried orange and lemon peels, liquorice root, angelica root, orris (the root of a certain iris plant) and coriander seed.

You can optionally switch on the still for a little while to warm it up and leave the contents to macerate, steeping like loose tea in the warm liquid to extract as much flavour as possible. This can take anywhere from 12 to 24 hours – the length of the maceration really depends on the size of the still, with a larger still requiring a longer maceration time.

When it is time to distil, the liquid is once again warmed slowly. Different compounds have different boiling points – this is the alchemy of distilling. The first liquid to come from the still is called the 'heads'. It is a group of compounds with boiling points lower than that of ethyl alcohol. These are carefully separated and discarded.

Next comes the beginning of the 'heart'. This is the beverage alcohol, the ambrosia of the distillation run. Different botanical notes come over the still at different points in the distilling of the heart. The citrus comes first, announcing the start with a burst of sweet orange and lemon that an experienced distiller can smell from across the room. In the middle of the heart, the juniper comes in abundance as refined pine aromas. This moment more than any other resembles the finished product, but gin is not complete without the earlier and later portions of the heart. Towards the end, the deeper flavours emerge – the savoury, earthy notes.

When the aroma becomes biscuity, toasty and creamy, it is time for the distiller to stop collecting the heart. The next flavour to come is surprisingly bready and the texture of the liquid becomes thick, feeling almost like lotion on your skin. Such is the difference between the heads, hearts and tails of a distillation.

After the heart has been collected, it needs to be cut to bottling strength. It comes off the still at over 80 per cent alcohol. Water is added to bring the spirit to bottling strength and then the spirit is essentially homogenised for a few weeks (mixed to keep it from settling into layers of different densities). Now, the gin is ready for bottling – and sipping.

THE KNOW HOW

One of the secrets of great drinks, whether you are following a recipe or experimenting with your own creations, is balance. That is what each recipe does – balancing strong against weak (spirit against dilution), sour against sweet (usually citrus against sugar) and modifying these further with spice (bitters or vermouth). These are the building blocks of a great drink. Too strong or too weak and a drink is not as good. Too sour or too sweet, and again it will not be as good as it could be. Follow these recipes, measure carefully, taste, and afterwards begin to shift the ratios to your own palate. A little more or less of each, a little more or less mixing time, a larger or smaller twist for garnish and you are making the same modifications the world's best bartenders make – except now it is you tailoring drinks to your own palate. In the next few pages, we outline the tools, techniques and ingredients used over the course of the book.

HOME BAR TOOLS

This is the essential kit for creating great cocktails at home (and what you can make do with at a pinch).

❶ MIXING GLASS – For stirring drinks. Mixing glasses are generally purpose-built for the task with a wide opening for large ice cubes and a pour spout. Just about any wide-mouthed pitcher would work, or even a large glass, beer mug or stein.

❷ BAR SPOON – A long-handled spoon for measuring ingredients and stirring. Wooden spoons work at a pinch, but use them the wrong way round for stirring.

❸ SHAKER – There are two common types: the two-part and the three-part. Two-part shakers are much easier to open after shaking. They are either a pair of metal 'tins' or one metal tin and one glass that fit together.

❹ HAWTHORNE STRAINER – A flat strainer adorned with a spring, it fits the top of a shaker tin and is used for straining shaken drinks. You can substitute a tea strainer, but it is a bit fiddly.

❺ JULEP STRAINER – Looking like a large spoon riddled with holes, it rests on top of the ice inside a mixing glass and is used for straining stirred drinks.

❻ FINE STRAINER – Used for double straining, to remove any small ice chips or bits of mint or fruit.

❼ JIGGER – This is a liquid measure, used to ensure that drinks are consistent. Just about any shotglass can work, providing you know how much liquid it holds.

❽ KNIFE AND CHOPPING BOARD – A small knife does well for cutting lemon and lime wedges and wheels.

❾ VEGETABLE PEELER – This is the best tool for cutting elegant lemon and orange twists and is far safer than using a knife for the job.

❿ 'MEXICAN ELBOW' – Fresh juice is always better than store-bought. Use a juicer to squeeze your fresh citrus juice.

⓫ STIRRER – Not essential, but an elegant stirrer is the perfect addition to any G&T.

GLASSWARE

There are no hard and fast rules about glassware, but certain drinks work better in certain glasses. Plus, there is lots of room for individuality here. Think of the following as guidelines.

 SHOT GLASS – These can be tall and slender, or short and squat. Many double as jiggers (see page 18). The size varies a bit by country. In the UK, the standard single shot is 25ml or 35ml. In the United States, a single is 1½oz or 44ml. Glassware in both countries tends to conform to these sizes.

CHAMPAGNE FLUTE/COUPE – There are two styles of Champagne glass. The flute tends to preserve the fizz better than a coupe, but the material comes into play as well. Crystal glasses are not as smooth as those made of glass. Imperfections in crystal give carbonation points on which bubbles form and break out of solution, floating up to the top.

 COCKTAIL GLASS – Also referred to as a Martini glass. These days there are two basic shapes: the classic V and the coupette, which, as the name implies, is a small coupe. There is no qualitative difference between the two, and both should contain around 120ml.

NICK & NORA GLASS – With a bowl shaped in a half-sphere, the Nick & Nora takes its name from glassware used in the *Thin Man* film series, based on Dashiell Hammett's 1934 novel.

 WHITE WINE GLASS – For cocktails, a white wine glass is an elegant substitute for a rocks glass or tumbler.

RED WINE GLASS – This stemmed wine glass with a large bowl makes a lovely alternative for highball drinks that include spirit, mixer and ice.

GIN JULEP CUP – A julep cup is a singular entity, as it is rarely used for any drink other than a julep. Traditionally made of silver, silver-plate or pewter, today, julep cups are also made from steel or are even copper plated. The exterior tends to become frosty when a properly made julep is inside.

ROCKS GLASS – Short and broad with a flat bottom, it is sometimes referred to as a tumbler or Old Fashioned glass (because it is the glass for an Old Fashioned cocktail). These vary widely in size, as there are single and double rocks glasses. The rocks glass takes its name from a nickname for ice: rocks.

HIGHBALL GLASS – A tall, narrow glass which usually contains 250ml to 350ml. The name is said to come from the American railways, where the signal for clear tracks ahead was a 'highball' – a metal ball hoisted high and easily visible to the train drivers. According to legend, bartenders near the tracks served whiskey or gin and soda with a couple of ice cubes which would rise to the top, mimicking the all-clear symbol.

COLLINS GLASS – Slightly taller and narrower than a highball glass, a classic collins glass has a singular elegance to it. As the shape is so close, it is interchangeable with a highball glass.

HOME COCKTAILING TECHNIQUES

The recipes in this book will require a few different techniques – here's our how-to. Master these, and you'll soon be making great, expertly crafted drinks.

 CHILL – If you keep your cocktail glasses in a cabinet, then the first step in making a drink is to fill the glasses with ice and water to chill them. Ice alone will not chill them. Adding water ensures 100 per cent contact between the ice and the glass, taking the heat out of the glass. If you put your glasses in the freezer, leave them there until the drinks are mixed. Either way, chilling is essential, because pouring a drink into a warm glass will spoil the drink.

STIR – Fill the mixing glass at least halfway with ice. If you add the ice before the liquid, it will not be as likely to splash. How long you stir your cocktail for depends on the ice quality. Very cold, hard ice requires a longer stir to attain the desired dilution to open up the flavours. This is usually around 25 per cent dilution. Ice chips might require as little as 15 seconds. Hand-carved, tempered ice could take up to 90 seconds.

 BUILD – Some drinks, such as the French 75 or Gin & Tonic, are created directly in the glass they will be served in. This is called 'building'.

LIFT – To mix fizzy drinks, do not stir with a circular motion. Instead, reach the bar spoon to the bottom of the glass and then lift it back out. Once or twice should be sufficient to mix the drink while preserving the carbonation.

SHAKE – Fill the shaker about halfway with ice. Add the drink ingredients. Close the shaker firmly and hold it so you are grasping both parts – you do not want them to separate while you are shaking. As with the stirring technique (opposite), how long you shake for depends on the quality of the ice.

THROW – This mixing technique may sound difficult, but it is easier than stirring. Fill a shaker tin with ice right to the top. Add the drink ingredients. Place a julep strainer over the ice. Holding the tin in one hand, with a finger firmly on the strainer to keep it in place, raise it above your head with an empty tin in your other hand. Begin pouring from the full tin to the empty one. As you do, lower the hand with the empty one and let the liquid fall increasingly far before it is caught in the lower tin. Then bring the tins together and pour the liquid back in over the julep strainer. Repeat. If you want to keep your shoes dry, only watch the catching vessel and never look at your throwing hand. This technique gives more sustained aeration than shaking, with the clarity of stirring.

 STRAIN – Use a julep or Hawthorne strainer to hold back the ice and let the drink pour into the glass. Just make sure the strainer is held firmly in place on the shaker or in the mixing glass before you begin to pour through it.

 DOUBLE STRAIN – After shaking a drink and pouring it through a Hawthorne strainer (as above), you can then pour it through a tea strainer to remove any small ice chips or bits of mint or fruit. This is also sometimes referred to as 'fine straining'.

GIN-LOVER'S LARDER

Keep a few essentials in the cupboard or refrigerator, and you'll be able to whip up a great cocktail in no time. Here's our list of must-haves – not forgetting the gin of course!

ICE – This is the key to any great cocktail. Fresh ice from filtered water makes better-tasting drinks. As you will likely need more than you expected, it's a good idea to buy at least one bag of ice before inviting people for drinks. Note that if the ice is kept in the freezer until it is put into the shaker or mixing glass (as opposed to keeping it in an ice bucket), it will stay colder. This will not actually make the drinks colder since you can only bring the temperature down to a few ticks above freezing, but it will take longer to gain the drink dilution you want.

SIMPLE SYRUP – Also known as sugar syrup or gomme syrup, this is made by combining equal parts of sugar and water (some bartenders will quickly point out that gomme syrup also contains gomme arabic, giving it a slightly different mouthfeel). You can buy it as gomme syrup or cane syrup in most shops, or you can quickly and easily make your own (see page 26).

LEMONS, LIMES AND ORANGES – Fresh citrus is crucial and if you have one of these ripe and ready in the larder you are in a good place. Fruit can be cut before drinks are served, but not days before. Leftover twists and wedges should not be saved for use the next day; they quickly get stale and drinks amplify the flavour of the garnish.

CHERRIES – Maraschino cherries were not always bright red and artificially flavoured. Thankfully, high-quality cherries, such as Luxardo from Italy and Somerset Cider Brandy Cherries, are becoming widely available.

ANGOSTURA BITTERS – Bitters is to the bar what salt is to the kitchen. A couple of dashes of Angostura bitters brings complexity to a drink, with a range of flavours from bright grapefruit notes to earthy and warm spices.

ORANGE BITTERS – You really only ever need two types of bitters and this is the other one. Its bitter orange flavour was present in the first ever Martini and Dry Martini recipes, as well as countless other drinks.

VERMOUTH – For Martinis, you need dry vermouth (not bianco or white vermouth). For many other drinks you need sweet (a.k.a. red) vermouth. Most importantly, you need fresh vermouth. Vermouth is a wine – about the same ABV (alcohol by volume) as a good Bordeaux wine, it breathes, then rots and dies, just like a good Bordeaux would if you kept it in the drinks cabinet for months after opening it. Today, many shops stock half bottles, and even mini bottles. Once opened, vermouth should be kept in the refrigerator.

TRIPLE SEC – Essentially a citrus substitute for simple syrup, it is used in drinks such as the White Lady (see page 83).

SIMPLE SYRUP &
FRESH SOUR MIX

Many recipes call for simple syrup, or for a combination of simple syrup and fresh lemon or lime juice. This light, simple combination replaces the dreadful, store-bought 'sour mix' that used to regularly drive people away from cocktails and back to prosecco and pints. However, you can easily pre-mix fresh citrus and simple syrup to make a fresh sour mix which will impress even the most finicky cocktail drinkers.

MAKING SIMPLE SYRUP: You can heat water on the stovetop or in a kettle and then combine it with an equal measure of sugar to create simple syrup (1 part sugar and 1 part water will make about 1.5 parts simple syrup, so if you want to make 400ml simple syrup, combine 250g sugar with 250ml water). However, even if you combine them without heating the water, the sugar will eventually dissolve. It might take 20 minutes at room temperature versus 3 minutes over a low heat, but once it is dissolved, it will stay that way. Shops also sell simple syrup, often labelled gomme syrup or cane syrup.

MAKING FRESH SOUR MIX: To make 500ml fresh sour mix, freshly squeeze 250ml of citrus juice (lemon or lime depending on the drinks you want to make), then combine with an equal measure of simple syrup.

GARNISHES

You might think of them as the icing on the cake (or the parsley on the steak), but drink garnishes play a much more central role than simply adding colour. A garnish can have a huge impact on the flavour of a drink. This is why good bars ensure their garnishes are cut fresh for service each day, and great bars tend to cut their garnishes fresh for each drink. While a few garnishes – lemon twist, cherry, lime wedge – adorn the vast majority of drinks, there is a whole world of garnishes worth exploring.

Citrus

Citrus fruit has three distinct flavours: the peel, the pulp and the pith. The peel with its pores loaded with citrus oils carries floral and sweet citrus aromas and a sharp but clean, bitter taste. The pulp gives the fresh and sour-flavoured juice. The pith, the white tissue between the peel and the pulp, is dry and bitter and really only shines in marmalade.

LEMON – Look for organic and unwaxed fruit, if possible. If not, go with whatever you can get your hands on, as long as it is fresh.

LIME – The most common lime today is the Persian lime. However, a few of the classic recipes were born in times and places where the key lime or Mexican lime dominated. These smaller and sweeter limes are lovely and worth a try if you can find them.

ORANGE – Oranges don't get used quite as much as lemons for garnish, but they are very easy to work with and bring a gentler flavour to a drink, so we enjoy using them. In season, blood oranges are a delicious substitute.

GRAPEFRUIT – With few exceptions, only grapefruit twists or half wheels are used in drinks. However, you can cut a hybrid of the two by using a knife to cut a twist, cutting it a bit too deep so that a bit of pulp remains attached. This also works for the orange garnish in a Negroni.

POMELO – The biggest of the citrus fruits and mostly pith inside, its twist gives a flavour similar to grapefruit.

BERGAMOT – For years, the only supply we could find popped up in the Amsterdam market in January and February, then this enigmatic citrus (best known as the driving flavour in Earl Grey tea) would disappear once again. Now, thankfully, it is becoming more widely available. It is pricey, but has an intense flavour, so a little goes a long way in a drink. If you are using the juice, for example, you can use 1 part bergamot to 3 or 4 parts lemon juice. The twists give a powerful and fascinating aroma.

CUTTING TWISTS: The perfect citrus twist is large and very thin, with a minimum of white pith on the back. There are two ways to cut them: the horrible but economical way and the perfect but rather wasteful way (you can guess which we prefer).

To get the most possible twists from a lemon, cut the ends off and hollow it out with a bar spoon. Then, cut the hollow barrel-shaped lemon in half and then into a bunch of twists. They will have a lot of pith attached.

Our preferred method is to use a vegetable peeler to shave off a broad thin peel with a minimum of pith, working from one end of the fruit to the other. You might get half a dozen twists from a lemon versus about 30 awful little morsels with the other method, but these twists can be squeezed elegantly over the drink to express a veritable cloud of sweet citrus oils.

The twist should be held gently, so it does not prematurely release the oil from its pores. Hold it over the drink and squeeze once, with the skin-side facing down. You should now be able to see droplets of oil on top of the drink. Remember, a twist can only be squeezed once. After that, the pores in the peel have given their all and the twist is merely decorative. It still carries oils on its surface, and these will add a bitter taste to a drink if you put the twist in after squeezing it over. Thus, for some drinks, our recommendation is to squeeze and discard.

Citrus twists can be tied into all sorts of fancy shapes for a decorative garnish, but this doesn't mean you should ever do it to a twist you plan to use to impart flavour. If the twists are squeezed on a chopping board while tying them up, their flavour ends up on the board rather than the drink.

SQUEEZING CITRUS JUICE: While citrus juice is an ingredient rather than a garnish, it is natural to mention it here as you can peel the twists off a piece of fruit, then split it in half across the middle and use a 'Mexican elbow' or other citrus juicer to extract the juice for cocktails.

CUTTING WEDGES: Normally, only lemons and limes get cut into wedges for cocktails. When cutting anything, safety is most important. With that in mind, if you cut the fruit in half lengthways, you can lay each half cut-side down. With the fruit flat, it is easy to split each half lengthways into four wedges.

CUTTING WHEELS & HALF WHEELS: For wheels, cut across the fruit rather than lengthways. For half wheels, cut the fruit lengthways and lay the halves cut-side down. Now, cutting them into half wheels is quick and simple. This is especially good for oranges and grapefruit.

Briny flavours

OLIVES – Whether you are hungry or simply craving a touch of salt, olives are a great garnish. Just know that there are a million varieties beyond the ones sold next to the maraschino cherries and, while those are the only ones labelled 'cocktail olives', they may be about the lowliest choice. We highly recommend experimenting with different types of olives and, if you're a fan of dirty Martinis, with different forms of olive brine. Keep your olives in the refrigerator. You can even move them to the freezer for a few hours before the guests arrive. A chilled garnish keeps the drink cold.

CAPER BERRIES – While capers, the unopened buds of the caper bush, can be used for a cocktail garnish, the caper berry, the fruit of the caper bush, is a much better shape and size and even comes with a handy stem. This is an underrated Martini garnish and can be used in a number of other drinks, especially if there is vermouth or sherry in the recipe.

ROCK SAMPHIRE – Samphire has been recognised for its delicious flavour for ages. Not the easiest ingredient to find, but it is becoming more common these days. The flavour will appeal to fans of dirty Martinis; it has a salty and pleasantly savoury taste, like a mild caper. Use it where a drink calls for an olive or the drink is savoury and not citrus-driven.

Fruits & berries

COCKTAIL CHERRIES – Those bright red cherries, in a colour that doesn't occur in nature, might have a vestigial appeal from childhood, but they're loaded with preservatives. Thankfully, they were only ever modernisations on far better cherries made by companies such as Luxardo from Northern Italy, and these classic cherries are now widely available. In truth, during cherry season, you can make cocktail cherries at home. It's not too difficult and there are lots of recipes online.

FRESH CHERRIES – In season, try a fresh cherry in place of a cocktail cherry. If you buy black cherries and slice them into a drink, they will impart a gorgeous colour as well.

RASPBERRIES – Raspberries are one of our favourite fruits to infuse in gin for the blush colour and just-picked aroma they impart (see Raspberry Gin Sling on page 170).

BLACKBERRIES – Indispensable for the Bramble (see page 99) and a few other cocktails, you can use them fresh or put them in the freezer overnight.

GOOSEBERRIES – Seldom seen in cocktail bars because of their limited availability, gooseberries give a lemony tartness if you slice them and perch a couple of slices on the rim of a drink.

CURRANTS – Redcurrants are the most common in bars, usually in a cluster with the stem still attached. Feel free to use redcurrants in or on a drink where a lemon or orange twist is called for. Squeeze the twist over the drink, discard it and garnish with the currants instead.

Spices

STAR ANISE – This dark, wood-toned and star-shaped seed pod comes from evergreen trees native to Vietnam and China. It gives a lovely anise aroma in the nose, but needs heat and time to release its taste. This works well, as it could otherwise dominate a drink.

CLOVES – The easiest way to garnish with cloves is to embed them in a bit of citrus, such as an orange half-wheel. Use a kebab skewer to puncture the orange rind and the cloves will easily slot into the holes.

CINNAMON STICK – Normally associated solely with hot drinks, it is not uncommon in Spain to find a cinnamon stick garnish in a Gin & Tonic.

NUTMEG – Nutmeg is always best freshly grated. Always do this over the drink once it is in the glass, as nutmeg is more essential to the aroma than the taste.

Other

RHUBARB – There are two ways to use rhubarb: as a raw stalk, cut so it is just a centimetre or two taller than the glass, or as a lightly cooked chunk. If you are using it raw, you can (and should) slice it lengthways into at least two if not three pieces, to create a slimmer and more manageable stalk. For a cooked piece, we roast chunks of rhubarb with sugar and vanilla pods, then store them in the freezer. A frozen chunk melts and softens without warming the drink and adds a beautiful hint of rhubarb flavour to the drink.

CELERY – Most associated with the Bloody Mary and Red Snapper, celery found its way into these drinks in the 1960s, at the Ambassador East Hotel in Chicago, when it was added as a substitute for the swizzle stick.

MINT SPRIG – Almost entirely associated with sweet and citrus-based drinks, a mint sprig is best paired with a cut-short straw, so that the person sipping the drink does so with their nose in the mint.

MINT LEAF – Used on short drinks, a single large mint leaf can be awakened for a burst of mint aroma by 'spanking' it. Cup the leaf in the palm of one hand and firmly clap over it once with your other cupped hand without actually hitting the leaf. The abrupt increase in air pressure between your hands will release the flavoursome oils from the tiny hairs on the leaf, wafting the aroma into the air. Do it where the drink is served for best results.

BASIL LEAF – A single large basil leaf makes a lovely, aromatic garnish, but there are some lesser-known varieties that make for fun experimentation. A Greek basil sprig is striking and delicious. Shiso – often referred to as Japanese basil – is part of the mint family. The leaves are large and give a burst of fresh flavour. It balances well with citrus or with wine-modified drinks, such as the Martini.

SALT & SUGAR – To coat the rim of a glass with salt or sugar, cover a small plate or shallow dish with sugar or salt. Wet the rim of the glass by rubbing a citrus wedge around it. Then set the glass upside-down onto the plate. If this doesn't get as much on as you'd like, roll the rim of the glass slowly across the plate. Many drinks calling for a salt rim will taste even better if you put a little sugar in the salt. Try to avoid iodised salt for cocktail rims.

TO FINISH, a few of the oddest garnishes we have encountered over the years: grilled octopus tentacle, tiny grilled squid, a slice of crisp streaky bacon, a garlic-stuffed olive, a hazelnut marinated in maraschino liqueur, an anchovy-stuffed olive, a blue-cheese-stuffed olive, a kumquat, a lychee, edible flowers... It's an endless list and loads of fun to explore. Happy experimenting!

The *Cocktails*

ONE GIN, ONE HUNDRED COCKTAILS

What do the majority of classic cocktails have in common?
They are made with only two or three ingredients. The
Martini, Manhattan, Daiquiri, Margarita, Gin & Tonic,
Rob Roy, Old Fashioned, Tom Collins, White Lady, the list
goes on. To become a classic, a drink must be simple and
universally replicable. Good spirits and one or two good
modifiers is what it takes to make a great drink. That's all it
takes – more or less – to master the drinks in this book.
Some of them have been passed down through the ages,
others were born in the last few decades, and still others are
hot-off-the-press, with a few created solely for this book.

What these hundred drinks have in common is a single gin:
classic London Dry Gin. There's a great reason why all those
other gin styles – cream of the valley, table gin, cordial gin,
and so on – faded away in the mid-1800s. London Dry Gin's
smooth and balanced feel, and its distinct pine and citrus
flavour vaulted it to the top of all the spirits categories. It
pairs with a surprising number of flavours, from sweet and

fruity to bracing and citrus, from savoury and salty to wine and even cream. We selected the following drinks, first because they are personal favourites and second because they show off the range of flavours in our handcrafted gin.

We have grouped recipes here and there by occasion, selecting a few of the ones that best fit. So, if you're looking for the easiest, the best for a sweltering summer's day, for the fireside, or the newest of the new, flip through. If you are not familiar with the mixing techniques, or want more info on the tools and ingredients in the recipes, check the Know How section on pages 16–33.

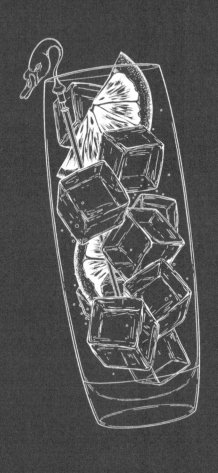

REALLY SIMPLE

Not yet convinced that you can mix drinks at home?
Or want to enjoy time with your guests and your
drinks rather than spending the entire evening
in the kitchen mixing them? Let's start simple
then with these five recipes – easy, delicious and
endlessly sippable.

The *Fairfax*

'My three ingredients?' says Sipsmith founder Fairfax Hall. 'Gin, ice and a glass. If the gin is good, there's no reason to mask it with other ingredients.' More or less stirring makes this either a soft or a bracing drink. In truth, with our gin, you don't even need to stir – you can pour and just let it sit and mellow for a while.

🍸 50ml Sipsmith London Dry Gin
🍸 Ice

Fill a rocks glass or tumbler with ice. Add gin. Enjoy.

Not all drinks need to be garnished. A garnish can bring essential flavour to a drink and can enhance the appearance, but it can just as easily add unnecessary flavour and get in the way, detracting from the experience. Thus, garnishes are nice, but not required.

Gin & Tonic

Quite likely, this drink was born in London on 26 June 1858, when Pitt's Aerated Quinine Tonic Water began an advertising campaign to convince the public that their new drink would replace the soda, with a little brandy added, recommended by doctors as your daily drink. At least, this is what their ads stated. Sadly, they missed a trick by recommending brandy with their tonic. Predictably, it was a non-starter in London. But this was a new world of opportunities and soon Pitt's Aerated Tonic Water ventured as far afield as New Zealand, Singapore and India. Within ten to fifteen years, visitors and returning ex-pats from the colonies, especially India, lamented that they couldn't find England's most famous drink (as they knew it) in the heart of England. It didn't take long for canny pub landlords to begin offering Gin & Tonics.

As for the garnish? The traditional ones are a slice of lemon or a lime wedge. However, a lemon twist is lovely. A bit of grapefruit works. A rosemary sprig? Why not!

- 50ml Sipsmith London Dry Gin
- 100–150ml tonic water

To garnish: A lime wedge or garnish of your choosing.

Combine the ingredients in an ice-filled highball glass. Garnish with anything that takes your fancy. The Sipsmith favourite is a lime wedge.

Gin & It

Effortless to make and delicious, legend has it that this was the Queen Mother's favourite tipple. She is said to have consumed them consistently at the Savoy's American Bar over the decades. This streamlined version of a Sweet Martini on the Rocks is more like a Gin Manhattan than a Martini, and, thankfully, has a much simpler name than 'Gin Manhattan on the Rocks with an Orange Slice'. The bitters are optional, so don't worry if you haven't got them handy.

- 45ml Sipsmith London Dry Gin
- 45ml sweet vermouth
- 2 dashes of orange bitters (optional)

To garnish: An orange half wheel

Combine the ingredients in an ice-filled rocks glass or tumbler. Stir. Garnish with the orange.

Nutmeg graters were the original bling. In 18th-century England, nutmeg cost more than its weight in gold, so flashy folks determined to flaunt their wealth wore silver nutmeg graters on chains around their necks. They would also bring their own nutmeg into restaurants and gin palaces.

Gin *Sangaree*

Gin and port. It works so well. An archaic word for sangria, the Sangaree was around before the cocktail, dating back to the 1700s. By the mid-1800s, it came to mean a mixed drink with port.

- 50ml Sipsmith London Dry Gin
- 10ml simple syrup (see page 26)
- 25ml port

To garnish: Freshly grated nutmeg (optional)

Combine the gin and simple syrup in an ice-filled rocks glass (crushed ice looks especially pretty). Stir, then layer on the port to finish. Optional: grate a little nutmeg over the top to garnish.

If you prefer, you can stir this drink in a mixing glass and strain it into a chilled cocktail glass. It has been served both ways for nearly two centuries (before that, ice was a rare novelty).

Gin *Rickey*

While Gin & Tonics are lovely, sometimes it is nice to taste gin minus tonic's sugar and bitters. Colonel Joe Rickey, a Washington senator and bon vivant, created a simple drink of whiskey and soda with the juice of half a lime. By the mid-1890s, a gin version eclipsed his original and became one of the top-selling gin drinks in North America, until Prohibition hit in 1920. It nearly saw a resurgence in recent years except that modern bartenders overlooked an essential bit of history. This drink calls for 'the juice of half a lime', but in 1890s Washington DC, they were not using modern Persian limes, but rather Mexican or key limes, which are considerably smaller. This is also as low in calories as a Vodka Tonic, but with considerably more flavour.

- 50ml Sipsmith London Dry Gin
- 100ml sparkling or soda water
- 2 lime wedges

Combine the gin and soda in an ice-filled highball glass. Squeeze the lime wedges into the drink and drop them in.

CLASSICS

They say that everyone needs to know how to cook ten dishes. And when it comes to gin drinks, there are also a few you really should know. They're classics because they have stood the test of time, appealing to successive generations. They became universal. Say 'Martini please' at the Hotel Mamounia in Marrakesh and the bartender will make you one (a rather good one, in fact). Classics proliferate because the ingredients are universal and, more importantly, because they are simple. Here, we've chosen a selection of our favourite classic gin serves alongside some classics that we think taste better when made with gin. We're also giving you a bit more background on these because it's as important to understand the when, where and why, as it is the how.

Dry *Martini*

The most storied of all cocktails, today's Martini bears little resemblance to the complex drink born in or around the early 1880s. The first proper recipe, in Harry Johnson's *New Improved Illustrated Bartenders Guide*, used equal parts gin and sweet vermouth, plus such extras as absinthe, Curaçao and gomme syrup. Plus, it was garnished with a cherry. Today's Martini was really born in the early 1950s, when bartenders dispensed with the orange bitters and reduced the mix to its two fundamentals: gin and dry vermouth.

The secrets to making a good Martini are simple: use the best possible gin and a fresh bottle of vermouth. Use fresh ice and make sure your glass is ice-cold. Pay attention to the dilution you are introducing while stirring with the ice – 25 per cent is a good amount for opening up the flavours while maintaining the intensity. With ice from the supermarket, this should be achieved with 20–30 seconds of stirring. Garnish with a lemon twist or olive – Jared's favourite is a lemon twist expressed over the drink and discarded.

🍸 50ml Sipsmith London Dry Gin
🍸 10-25ml dry vermouth

To garnish: A lemon twist or olive

Combine the ingredients in an ice-filled mixing glass. Stir. Strain into a chilled Martini glass. Garnish and enjoy.

Olives and twists are not mutually exclusive. If a drink calls for an olive garnish, you can squeeze a twist over the drink to add a touch of fresh citrus, but you might want to add an extra olive or a touch of brine as citrus reduces our perception of salinity.

Negroni

After the Martini and the Gin & Tonic, this obscure bartenders' favourite has risen in recent years to become the third most-popular of all the gin drinks. Even in Italy, they say you have to drink a few of them before you can hope to enjoy a Negroni. The Campari does have a sharp, grapefruit-peel flavour to it that can overwhelm the uninitiated palate. But it is worth persevering. This drink embodies the aperitivo concept, getting the digestive juices flowing before a meal.

Although it doesn't fit with the three-ingredient drinks in this book, our favourite Negroni is the Sloe Negroni, made with 4 equal measures: Sipsmith Sloe Gin, Sipsmith London Dry Gin, Campari and sweet vermouth. Countless bartenders have attempted to improve on the Negroni over the decades since its birth. Many of the variations are palatable, even pleasant, but all are just variations. At least, until we added sloe gin to the equation. Like any good ingredient, it loses its individual identity and brings out the best in the others. Suddenly, the Campari is wearing a red velvet smoking jacket, the vermouth has a couple of grand in its pocket, and the gin? The gin is nestled into a green leather Chesterfield, wearing an ascot and a smug expression. That's what a measure of sloe gin brings to a Negroni.

𝄞 25ml Sipsmith London Dry Gin
𝄞 25ml Campari
𝄞 25ml sweet vermouth

To garnish: An orange twist or wedge

Combine the ingredients in an ice-filled rocks glass or tumbler. Stir. Garnish with an orange twist or wedge.

Silver *Bullet*

Tracing back to the 1920s, this mix of juniper and caraway is loaded with spice. This is the perfect drink for the replete iconoclast, for the non-conformist. Plus, it is actually quite tasty.

- 50ml Sipsmith London Dry Gin
- 15ml kümmel liqueur
- 20ml fresh lemon sour mix (see page 26)

To garnish: A lemon twist

Combine the ingredients in an ice-filled cocktail shaker. Shake. Strain into a chilled cocktail glass. Squeeze a twist over the drink and discard the twist.

Army & Navy

Originally described as a drink that tastes a lot more expensive than it is, making it perfect when guests drop in, the Army & Navy combines the almond flavour of the orgeat and the lemon to bring out the best in the gin. This drink was named in reference to a football game between the US Army and Navy, probably during Prohibition, although the recipe first emerged in 1937. It was invented by New York advertising and public relations executive Carroll Van Ark (his daughter Joan starred as Valene Ewing in the 1980s soap opera *Knots Landing*). He frequently entertained guests at such landmarks as The Rainbow Room, the Waldorf Astoria and The Lexington Hotel, and was renowned for his cocktail parties at home.

- 50ml Sipsmith London Dry Gin
- 25ml orgeat syrup, or simple syrup (see page 26)
- 25ml fresh lemon juice

Combine the ingredients in an ice-filled cocktail shaker. Shake well. Strain into a chilled cocktail glass.

Bee's *Knees*

The phrase 'bee's knees' preceded the drink as flappers' slang meaning 'peachy', 'the berries', or 'very nice', according to *The Flapper Dictionary* serialised in American newspapers in 1922. A 1929 article credits 'Mrs J J Brown of Denver and Paris, widow of the famous miner' with inventing the drink, describing it as a 'rather sweet combination with honey and lemon'. A little further digging into the identity of Mr Brown's widow reveals she is none other than The Unsinkable Molly Brown, the *Titanic* survivor immortalised on stage and screen. Her Parisian invention need not be overly sweet, and is one of the best gin drinks ever created. To make The Business, substitute fresh lime juice for the lemon juice and garnish with a lime twist.

- 50ml Sipsmith London Dry Gin
- 25ml fresh lemon juice
- 20ml honey syrup*

Combine the ingredients in an ice-filled cocktail shaker. Shake well. Strain into a chilled cocktail glass.

* Honey syrup is a 50:50 mix of honey and water – it helps the honey dissolve easily into your drink; use it in your tea as well.

Tom *Collins*

Looking for a simple, refreshing long drink? This is it. Looking for a strange tale from the 1870s? This is also it. Debate still rages as to the origins of the Tom Collins. Was it at the Limerick in London? Perhaps. What is certain is that when it reached the States, it became the Great Tom Collins Hoax of 1874.

An innocent hick walks into a Manhattan bar. One of the regulars asks his name. On hearing it, the local replies with a gasp, 'Oh, so you're the one! There was a man in here just a few minutes ago named Tom Collins. He said the most horrible things about you. You should be able to catch him in the bar down the street'. On bursting into the next bar, loudly demanding to see Tom Collins, the hick would be sent on to the next and then the next and the next bar, until some kindly local would offer to end it in exchange for a round of drinks. Even the newspapers were in on it, as journalists spent a lot of time in bars (as they tend to now). Articles about the rogue Tom Collins proliferated.

- 50ml Sipsmith London Dry Gin
- 50ml fresh lemon sour mix (see page 26)
- 100ml soda water

To garnish: A lemon wheel or a lemon and cherry flag (see below)

Combine the ingredients in an ice-filled highball glass, or a slightly narrower collins glass. Garnish with a lemon wheel or a 'flag' – a lemon wheel and cherry held together with a cocktail stick.

Cosmopolitan

Taste this next to its namesake vodka-cranberry drink and there is no question that this one is better. It was also born many years before the drink that lubricated the 1990s. We first discovered this drink in *The Pioneers of Mixing at Elite Bars* by the American Traveling Mixologists. This group, whose identities are lost to history, joined together to record pre-Prohibition recipes in the hope that some day their nation would see sense again. It was published just after the Repeal, in 1934. With gin instead of vodka and raspberries instead of cranberry juice, you might expect a completely different drink. Yet it is remarkably similar.

- 50ml Sipsmith London Dry Gin
- 45ml fresh lemon sour mix (see page 26)
- 10ml triple sec

To garnish: 4–5 fresh raspberries

Set aside one raspberry. Combine all the remaining ingredients including the garnish in an ice-filled cocktail shaker. Shake well. Strain into a chilled cocktail glass. Garnish with the reserved raspberry.

Pink *Gin*

Not to be confused with the recent rash of fruity roseate gins crowding supermarket shelves, this rather savoury mixture is a true British classic. In the days before pubs stocked ice (if you wanted iced drinks you went to an 'American Bar'), there were water jugs along each bar top. And bitters dashers, too. Take your glass of straight gin from the barmaid, add bitters and cold water to your liking and this was the original 'pinkers' beloved by sailors and dock workers. Sir Francis Chichester, the first person to successfully circumnavigate the globe solo in a sailboat (say that ten times fast!), credited his success to a daily pink gin. This classic is even better if you keep the gin in the freezer.

- 50ml Sipsmith London Dry Gin
- 100ml very cold water
- 2–3 dashes of Angostura bitters

Combine the ingredients in a chilled cocktail glass or empty tumbler.

see overleaf >

Parisian *Nights*

If you're looking for a drink to please everyone, this is it. It's easy to love as it comes across with rich berry flavours, yet underneath it all, it is undeniably a classic Dry Martini. Created in 1920s Paris for stage and silent screen star Yvonne Arnaud, it is also simple to mix – it consists of three equal measures. You will find this drink mislabelled as the 'Arnaud Cocktail' across the internet. Call it whatever you like, it is simply delicious.

- 40ml Sipsmith London Dry Gin
- 40ml dry vermouth
- 40ml crème de cassis

To garnish: An orange twist

Combine the ingredients in an ice-filled mixing glass. Stir. Strain into a chilled cocktail glass. Garnish with an orange twist.

see overleaf >

Aviation

In the mood for something floral and citrus, but not sweet and fruity? This salute to the pioneers of aviation emerged in 1911, and then was lost and forgotten for decades before re-emerging as a cult favourite among the world's bartenders. It can be made with two types of violet liqueur (crème d'Yvette and crème de violette). However, it is even better with just three ingredients, with a roll of Parma Violets on the side.

♣ 50ml Sipsmith London Dry Gin
♣ 10ml fresh lemon juice
♣ 10ml crème d'Yvette

10ml crème de violette (optional)

To serve: A maraschino cherry and a roll of Parma Violets sweets

---

Combine the ingredients in an ice-filled cocktail shaker. Shake well. Strain into a chilled cocktail glass. Garnish with a maraschino cherry and serve with a roll of Parma Violets on the side.

Dirty *Martini*

Who first put that spoonful of olive brine into a Martini? Some suggest it was Franklin Delano Roosevelt, whom Churchill described as a sloppy but enthusiastic mixer. That's all it takes to make a Dirty Martini, but there are so many variations to explore. Our own Distiller, Ben, loves a bit of salt water in place of the olive brine. It makes sense – the brine is adding a touch of salt, something bartenders are just discovering as a new secret ingredient (try a little pinch in the Gimlet on page 78, for example – so good!). You can also pour out half the brine from a jar of olives, replace it with dry vermouth and leave it in the refrigerator for a week, then use this mixture in your Martini. This improves both the brine and the olives.

🌶 50ml Sipsmith London Dry Gin
🌶 15ml dry vermouth
🌶 5–10ml brine from a jar of olives

To garnish: Olives

Combine the ingredients in an ice-filled mixing glass. Stir. Strain into a chilled cocktail glass. Garnish with olives.

Gibson

Yes, this is just a classic Dry Martini garnished with cocktail onions, but that seemingly minor change does make it an entirely different drink, a drink that has a special place in many people's hearts as an aperitif. That bit of onion and pickling spice filtering through the drink whets the appetite in a way no lemon twist could ever match. London bartender Marion Beke, creator of Gibson Bar, serves his with a side of pickled onions and mushrooms.

⚲ 50ml Sipsmith London Dry Gin
⚲ 20ml dry vermouth
⚲ 1 dash of orange bitters (optional)

To garnish: 2 cocktail onions

Combine the ingredients in an ice-filled mixing glass.
Stir. Strain into a chilled cocktail glass. Garnish with
2 cocktail onions threaded onto a cocktail stick.

Hanky *Panky*

'Why Ada, that's the real hanky panky!' remarked actor Charles Hawtry to Ada Coleman, bartender at the Savoy's American Bar, when she presented him with this drink some time around 1915. And the drink's name was born. If you know your British actors, you might confuse him with Charles Hawtry of *Carry On* fame. However, the latter Charles was such a fan of the original that he borrowed his name. This fresh and minty variation on a Sweet Martini or Gin Manhattan has proven to be a favourite for generations since then.

 30ml Sipsmith London Dry Gin
 30ml sweet vermouth
 5–10ml Fernet-Branca

To garnish: An orange twist

Combine the ingredients in an ice-filled mixing glass. Stir. Strain into a chilled cocktail glass. Garnish with an orange twist.

Bijou

One of the godfathers of cocktails, Harry Johnson, created this jewel using equal parts of the three ingredients some time in the late 19th century. If you like the herbaceous explosion of Chartreuse, this is the version for you. If, however, you want to bring a little subtlety to the drink, try New York bartender Dale Degroff's gin-heavy proportions, which we prefer. While most recipes call for drops and dashes of bitters and other ingredients, this simple version won out in our taste tests.

- 50ml Sipsmith London Dry Gin
- 25ml sweet vermouth
- 25ml Green Chartreuse

Combine the ingredients in an ice-filled mixing glass. Stir. Strain into a chilled Nick & Nora glass.

Alaska

This classic first appeared in Jacques Straub's 1913 cocktail book *Drinks*, featuring an Old Tom-style gin. By the 1930 publication of *The Savoy Cocktail Book*, Old Tom yielded to the growing popularity of London Dry Gin and the orange bitters were omitted altogether. However, the book does add a little background to this oddly named cocktail: 'So far as can be ascertained this delectable potion is NOT the staple diet of the Esquimaux. It was probably first thought of in South Carolina – hence its name.' We prefer this updated recipe using the best of 1913 and 1930.

- 50ml Sipsmith London Dry Gin
- 15ml Yellow Chartreuse
- 2 dashes of orange bitters

To garnish: A lemon twist

Combine the ingredients in an ice-filled cocktail shaker. Shake. Strain into a chilled cocktail glass (preferably a coupette). Squeeze a lemon twist over the drink and discard.

Improved *Gin Cocktail*

When Jerry Thomas released his second edition of *The Bar-Tender's Guide* in 1876, he added a new appendix of 'Improved' offerings in the gin, whiskey and brandy categories, adding one more ingredient into already beloved cocktails. While it was usually maraschino, absinthe or an orange liquor, we prefer a stone-fruit brandy, such as apricot brandy, to allow the floral and citrus notes of gin to shine.

- 50ml Sipsmith London Dry Gin
- 10ml apricot brandy
- 2 dashes of Abbott's Bitters (or other aromatic bitter that is not Angostura bitters)

To garnish: A long grapefruit peel twist

Combine the ingredients in an ice-filled mixing glass. Stir. Strain into a rocks glass with 1 or 2 ice cubes. Garnish with a 'horse's neck' of grapefruit peel – a long, curling twist pressed to the inside of the glass so it spirals around in there.

Orange *Martini*

First published in the 1930 *Savoy Cocktail Book*, this cocktail highlights the best part of the orange – its fragrant rind – by steeping the garnish in the drink for about two hours.

- 🥄 25ml Sipsmith London Dry Gin
- 🥄 25ml dry vermouth
- 🥄 10ml sweet vermouth

To garnish: Pared peel of ¼ orange

Combine the ingredients and garnish in an empty mixing glass and let them steep for about 2 hours. Add ice. Stir. Strain into a chilled cocktail glass (preferably a coupette or a Nick & Nora glass).

We suggest multiplying this recipe and storing unused portions in the refrigerator for up to one month.

Gimlet

You could call this drink a Gin Daiquiri and they are siblings, as both trace back to the British Navy's rum and gin rations, which were doled out with lime juice, sugar and water. According to Raymond Chandler's 1953 Philip Marlow potboiler, *The Long Goodbye*, 'a real gimlet is half gin and half Rose's lime juice and nothing else'. Harry Craddock at the Savoy mixed his this way in the 1930s. While this is a lovely drink, earlier versions called for 'lime juice', and it is hard to beat fresh citrus.

- 50ml Sipsmith London Dry Gin
- 25ml fresh lime juice
- 20ml simple syrup (see page 26)

Combine the ingredients in an ice-filled cocktail shaker. Shake. Strain into a chilled cocktail glass.

You can use 25ml lime cordial in place of the fresh lime juice and simple syrup. Purists will tell you it is the only way to make a Gimlet.

Southside

Looking for a cult classic? This minted twist on the Gimlet requires no particular deftness or dexterity, just a momentary outburst of energy. Plus, it is best if you have a tea strainer handy. The idea is to give this drink a good hard shake so that the ice cubes break up the mint. Then, by double straining it, you get a faint green tinge with only the tiniest bits of mint in the drink.

- 50ml Sipsmith London Dry Gin
- 50ml fresh lime sour mix (see page 26)
- 6–10 fresh mint leaves

To garnish: A single mint leaf

Combine the ingredients in an ice-filled cocktail shaker. Shake well. Double strain into a chilled cocktail glass. Garnish with a mint leaf.

Gin *Buck*

The earliest-known food and spirits flavour pairing was gin and gingerbread. They were combined at London's 'Frost Fairs' as early as the winter of 1715–16 when the Thames froze. On the ice, a tent offering drinks made with geneva popped up near one offering gingerbread. By the 1730s, gin and gingerbread sellers walked London's streets with baskets of their wares. Hogarth included a gin and gingerbread seller as one of the central characters in his 1751 etching *Gin Lane*. And when the Thames froze hard enough for subsequent Frost Fairs, the river was dotted with gin and gingerbread tents. The first British book to contain cocktail recipes began with one combining gin and ginger. So, this combination strikes back to the beginnings of modern flavour pairings – mostly because it's awfully good.

🍸 50ml Sipsmith London Dry Gin
🍸 100ml ginger ale
🍸 25ml fresh lemon juice

To garnish: A lemon wedge

Combine the ingredients in an ice-filled highball glass. Lift rather than stir. Garnish with a lemon wedge.

If you add a whole lemon peel spiralled down between the ice and the inside of the glass (hint: put it in before the ice), the drink becomes a Horse's Neck. Substitute the lemon for lime and it becomes a Foghorn cocktail.

White *Lady*

Oranges and lemons. This cocktail is gin, citrus and more citrus – a lovely combination of fresh lemon juice and orange liqueur (triple sec or Cointreau). Created in 1919 by Harry MacElhone, who would later become the Harry of Harry's New York Bar in Paris, this drink was the cause of a few fights early on, but not for the reasons you might expect. The UK Bartenders' Guild's 1934 trade magazine noted that a few professionals had come to fisticuffs over whether or not egg white should be added to this drink. An egg white makes the drink creamy and gives it a pleasantly foamy top, but it is truly up to the person drinking it. If you want egg white, by all means add it.

- 50ml Sipsmith London Dry Gin
- 25ml triple sec or Cointreau
- 20ml fresh lemon juice

Combine the ingredients in an ice-filled cocktail shaker. Shake. Strain into a chilled cocktail glass.

The *Bronx*

Want something Martini-esque, but with a big hit of fresh orange? This fresh and light(er) twist on the Martini emerged in pre-Prohibition New York or Philadelphia and spawned a stack of more or less complicated variations within the first decade of the 20th century. We prefer a Dry Bronx, but you can make a Sweet Bronx (use sweet vermouth instead of dry vermouth) or a Perfect Bronx (use equal half-measures of sweet and dry vermouths). You can further complicate this drink with a dash of orange bitters, but it really isn't necessary.

🍸 25ml Sipsmith London Dry Gin
🍸 25ml dry vermouth
🍸 25ml fresh orange juice

To garnish: An orange twist

Combine the ingredients in an ice-filled cocktail shaker. Shake well. Strain into a chilled cocktail glass. Garnish with an orange twist.

Gin *Fizz*

'Somebody mixes a drink which his grandfather knew under the homely appellation of a "John Collins", calls it a "Gin Fizz" and everybody wants the new drink,' wrote an astute journalist in 1881. Still, this alternate name for the John Collins has stood the test of time. One variation is the optional egg white that has become common in this drink. The combination of egg white and soda water creates a meringue-like foam which can stand higher than the rim of the glass. However, even without the egg, and by any name, this is a wonderfully refreshing drink.

🦢 50ml Sipsmith London Dry Gin

🦢 50ml fresh lemon sour mix (see page 26)

🦢 100ml soda water or sparkling water

1 egg white (optional)

To garnish: A lemon half wheel

Combine the gin and lemon sour mix in an ice-filled cocktail shaker (add the egg white now if you are going to). Shake well. Strain into a highball glass (some people like ice in this one, others prefer it without). Top with a little soda water at a time, as the drink will rise up. Garnish with a lemon half wheel.

Gin *Swizzle*

A favourite in Barbados in the late 1800s and early 1900s, there are scads of variations on this classic. Thankfully, there are also a few constants: the highball glass of crushed ice, the gin, the lime and the swizzle stick. The mechanics are simple: fill a highball glass with crushed ice, add the essential liquids – spirit, something sweet and perhaps something herbaceous – and then mix together with a swizzle stick. This is a small stick with blender-like branches at the end, cut from the aptly named swizzle stick tree (*Quararibea turbinata*). You can order a real swizzle stick online, or you can buy reusable metal versions. To swizzle, place your swizzle stick in the drink after the ingredients. Hold the stick between the palms of your hands and rotate the stick rapidly to spin.

- 50ml Sipsmith London Dry Gin
- 50ml fresh lime sour mix (see page 26)
- 2 dashes of Angostura bitters

Combine the ingredients in a highball glass filled with crushed ice. Swizzle. Serve with a straw.

Gin & *Dubonnet*

If you tried Dubonnet years ago, you may wince at the name of this drink. But today's Dubonnet is not the Dubonnet you remember. In a truly daring move, Dubonnet has been re-formulated using better wine. It is now truly delicious, and so is this drink. (If you never tried Dubonnet before, ignore all that and give this one a go.) Dubonnet is similar to a sweet vermouth, except that sweet vermouth, despite its colour, is made from white wine. Dubonnet is made with red wine and botanicals. This drink is similar to the Gin & It (*see* page 43) and it was also favoured by the Queen Mother. You can add a dash of Angostura bitters if you like, and/or top this with a splash of soda, but it's great as is.

🦪 25ml Sipsmith London Dry Gin
🦪 50ml Dubonnet Rouge

To garnish: An orange wheel

Combine the ingredients in an ice-filled rocks glass or tumbler. Stir. Garnish with an orange wheel.

The *Dog's Nose*

This forgotten Victorian classic was once all the rage and even made an appearance in Dickens' *The Pickwick Papers*. It is a savoury and complex drink and can be served hot or cold. Although it would commonly have been heated with a loggerhead (a red-hot poker), it is far safer to heat it in the microwave or on the stove.

🍸 25ml Sipsmith London Dry Gin
🍸 10ml dark treacle
🍸 100ml porter or stout

Combine the gin and treacle in an empty rocks glass or tumbler. Stir to loosen up the treacle. Add the porter and stir gently once more. Ice is not traditional in this drink, but you can add it after the gin and treacle, but before the porter, if you like.

If you want to serve this drink hot, combine the ingredients in a microwaveable mug, stir, and then heat until warmed through.

Mayfair

An elegant lost classic, this evokes images of genteel, smoky London members' clubs, where people dressed in full formal attire any night of the week for dinner and a bit of gambling, and where only the best was served.

- 40ml Sipsmith London Dry Gin
- 40ml fresh orange juice
- 10ml apricot brandy

To garnish: 1 clove

Rub the clove around the rim of a cocktail glass and discard the clove. If you break off the little ball at the top of the clove and use the now-concave tip, it is easier than it sounds. Combine the ingredients in an ice-filled mixing glass. Stir. Strain into the cocktail glass.

London *Mule*

While you might think the Moscow Mule (vodka, ginger beer and limes in a copper mug) gave birth to the gin version, it's far more likely that the 'inventors' of the Moscow Mule simply substituted vodka for the gin in the signature drink of the *Queen Mary* and *Laconia* ocean liners, which was gin, ginger beer and limes. But, of course, this flavour pairing goes back further to the gin and gingerbread of the 18th-century 'Frost Fairs' on the frozen Thames (*see* page 82). Ginger was literally a hot commodity, valued for its warming effects at the end of the Little Ice Age as much as for its flavour.

- 50ml Sipsmith London Dry Gin
- 100ml ginger beer
- 2 lime wedges

Combine the gin and ginger beer in an ice-filled highball glass or a rocks glass. Gently squeeze in the lime wedges, then drop them in. Dip in a bar spoon and lift to mix.

What do sloe gin, grenadine and maraschino cherries have in common? Nothing! Sadly, too many companies in decades past found it more economical to use artificial flavours and colours, and the differences between them faded away. Today, you can still find rather dismal grenadine and maraschino cherries, but you can also find a lot of outstanding ones, too. Grenadine is made from pomegranates and should taste like citrus and vanilla. Maraschino cherries made as they were over a century ago are now on the shelves in better shops around the world as well.

Gin *Manhattan*

Yes, this drink really did exist long ago. It was very good, too. Sadly, it is long forgotten, as is bartender Willy 'The Only William' Schmidt who was famous for these in Manhattan until he – and they – faded away at the end of the 19th century. It will appeal more to someone who appreciates a classic Manhattan than a classic Dry Martini – and to just about anyone who enjoys a good cocktail.

🍸 50ml Sipsmith London Dry Gin
🍸 25ml sweet vermouth
🍸 1 dash of Angostura bitters

To garnish: 1 maraschino cherry

Combine the ingredients in an ice-filled mixing glass. Stir. Strain into a chilled cocktail glass. Garnish with a maraschino cherry.

Bramble

One of the most quintessentially British of the modern classics, the Bramble was created in London in the 1980s by the city's father of modern bartending, Dick Bradsell, who is better known for another of his creations – the Espresso Martini. When he and another bartender were opening a bar called Fred's (because Fred, the other bartender, had the ready funds to pay for the bar), Dick took the Singapore Sling he had been making for years and dropped the Benedictine and soda water, leaving the gin, blackberry liqueur, lemon and sugar.

- 50ml Sipsmith London Dry Gin
- 50ml fresh lemon sour mix (see page 26)
- 10ml crème de mûre

To garnish: 2 blackberries or a lemon twist

Combine the gin and sour mix in an ice-filled cocktail shaker. Shake. Strain into an ice-filled rocks glass or a tumbler filled with crushed ice (a rolling pin and a sandwich bag will do the trick to crush it). Drizzle the crème de mûre over the top. Garnish with a couple of blackberries or a lemon twist.

Gin & *Lemon*

There was a time when Gin and Bitter was all the rage. Then, for some reason, the name fell out of fashion and bitter lemon was renamed as lemon tonic. Thus the drink, Gin and Bitter, became the slightly less clear Gin & Lemon, or Gin & Lemon Tonic.

🍸 50ml Sipsmith London Dry Gin
🍸 100–150ml lemon tonic water
🍸 2 orange wedges

Combine the gin and lemon tonic in an ice-filled highball glass. Squeeze one of the orange wedges into the drink and discard it. Lift to mix. Garnish the drink with the other orange wedge.

Vesper

Ian Fleming's personal twist on the Martini. A touch of vodka softens the herbaceous character of the gin and Lillet Blanc aperitif wine brings more citrus to the drink than the usual dry vermouth. The drink was created by his friend Ivor Bryce and appeared in Fleming's first book, *Casino Royale*, in 1953. Its name comes from a butler offering drinks by saying, 'Vespers are served,' in reference to the daily evening prayers in the Catholic church.

- 45ml Sipsmith London Dry Gin
- 15ml Sipsmith Sipping Vodka
- 7.5ml Lillet Blanc

To garnish: A large lemon twist

Combine the ingredients in an ice-filled mixing glass. Stir. Strain into a chilled Champagne coupe or a cocktail coupette. Garnish with a large lemon twist.

Perfect *Martini*

Back in the day, 'perfect' meant not dry or sweet but balanced between the two, at least when the word prefaced a Martini, Manhattan or Rob Roy. With people rediscovering the wonders of good vermouth, it is time to see this gem sparkle once again.

🍸 40ml Sipsmith London Dry Gin
🍸 20ml dry vermouth
🍸 20ml sweet vermouth

To garnish: A lemon twist

Combine the ingredients in an ice-filled mixing glass. Stir. Strain into a chilled cocktail glass. Garnish with a lemon twist.

A lemon twist imparts two different flavours to a drink. When you squeeze it over the top of a drink, it gives sweet, floral and citrus notes. When you run a twist around the rim of a glass or drop it into the drink, it adds a sharp hit of lemon bitters. There are times when you want both. Jared's favourite is a lemon twist squeezed over the Martini and discarded.

Orange *Blossom Special*

Long before Snoop Dogg was 'sippin' on gin and juice', the flappers and Bright Young Things of the 1920s were mixing up gin and orange with a touch of honey. This recipe made it so simple: dip a teaspoon into the honey and, still holding it vertically, set it into the cocktail shaker. You only need as much honey as sticks to the spoon, just a little bit.

- 50ml Sipsmith London Dry Gin
- 50ml fresh orange juice
- 1 bar spoon of honey

To garnish: An orange twist

Combine the ingredients in an ice-filled shaker. Shake well. Strain into a chilled cocktail glass and garnish with an orange twist.

Gin *Julep*

Trace back a bit in the history of the julep, particularly before the drink reached America, and it was not necessarily a whiskey drink. People made juleps out of just about any spirit and each had unique qualities. The Gin Julep is long-lost but worth rediscovering.

- 50ml Sipsmith London Dry Gin
- 15-20ml simple syrup (see page 26)
- 3-4 fresh mint sprigs

To garnish: Extra mint sprigs and a dusting of icing sugar (optional)

Combine the ingredients in a wine glass or a julep cup. Press the mint down lightly with a bar spoon a few times. Stir the ingredients together. Fill the cup with crushed ice. Garnish with more mint sprigs and, optionally, dust the top with icing sugar.

OCCASIONS

While a good cocktail can turn any idle hour into an occasion, some drinks are simply perfect for certain types of occasions. Here we have selected some of our favourite moments to raise a glass.

SUMMER SIPPING

Long, tall and quenching drinks are the order of the dog days. Thankfully, our species spent a lot more time existing without air conditioning than with it, and spent that time productively by coming up with loads of cooling summer drinks.

Summer *Fizz*

Wheat beer is an excellent and completely overlooked mixer. Unlike other beers, it tends not to have a prominent hoppy, sour edge, and so it balances well with sweet flavours, especially fruits.

- 25ml Sipsmith London Dry Gin
- 25ml crème de cassis or Chambord
- 100ml wheat beer

To garnish: An orange twist or fresh berries

Combine the ingredients in an ice-filled highball glass or wine goblet. Lift. Garnish with an orange twist or fresh berries.

Gin *Basil Smash*

Created by bartender Jörg Meyer in Hamburg, in 2008, this is a quintessential modern classic – so much so that it had to make it onto these pages. In the cocktail lexicon, the word 'smash' is a bit unclear – something about a drink including fruit in Victorian times. However, here it makes perfect sense as the basil gets pulverised like pesto, releasing a burst of flavour.

- 50ml Sipsmith London Dry Gin
- 7 fresh basil leaves
- 50ml fresh lemon sour mix (see page 26)

There are two ways to make this drink: Jörg's way and a less fussy, quick way.

Jörg's way: Set aside a single basil leaf. Place the remaining basil leaves and the lemon sour mix into a cocktail shaker. Muddle the basil: using the end of a wooden spoon (or a muddler if you have one), gently press and twist down on the basil to release its flavour. Add ice and gin. Shake well. Double strain into an ice-filled rocks glass or tumbler. Garnish with the reserved basil leaf.

And the quick way: Combine all the ingredients in an ice-filled cocktail shaker. Shake hard. Dump the contents, ice and all, into a tumbler or rocks glass and enjoy all the bits of shredded basil in the drink. Raise the glass toward Hamburg.

Rhubarb *Jammer*

Jams and jellies make excellent cocktail ingredients. Place a couple of spoonfuls into the cocktail shaker and you can toast with the taste you usually enjoy on toast.

- 50ml Sipsmith London Dry Gin
- 25ml rhubarb jam (about 5 teaspoons)
- 20ml fresh lemon juice

To garnish: A thin slice of raw rhubarb

Combine the ingredients in an ice-filled cocktail shaker. Shake well. Double strain (you can use the heel of the shaker to tap the tea strainer if it gets clogged by the jam) into a chilled rocks glass or jam jar. Garnish with a thin bit of rhubarb.

You can also serve this as a long drink. Skip the double strain. Skip the strain entirely. Shake briefly, then dump the contents, ice and all, into a highball glass or a jam jar. Garnish as before.

Salty *Dog*

An ideal drink for hotter climes. The essential salt rim can be made from Maldon Salt if you crush it a bit first, or any similar medium-flake salt. Fine granular salt works as well, as long as it is not iodised. There are loads of moments to get your daily intake of iodine; a Salty Dog is not one of them.

- 50ml Sipsmith London Dry Gin
- 100ml fresh golden grapefruit juice

To garnish: Salt

Wet the rim of a rocks glass with a bit of grapefruit juice or by running a wedge of grapefruit around the rim. Aim for a band about 5–10mm wide. Upturn the glass into a shallow dish of salt to coat the rim. Carefully add ice, gin and grapefruit juice to the glass. Stir gently.

Gin *Tommy's*

Rounded and refreshing, this one has soft hints of tequila from the agave syrup. Far better known as a tequila drink, invented at Tommy's in San Francisco, it works at least as well with gin.

- 50ml Sipsmith London Dry Gin
- 20ml fresh lime juice
- 10ml agave nectar

1 egg white (optional)

To garnish: A lime wheel

Combine the ingredients in an ice-filled cocktail shaker. Shake well. Strain into a chilled cocktail glass. Garnish with a lime wheel.

Optional: Add an egg white to the shaker for a frothy, creamy version.

Watermelon *Martini*

Watermelon is so simple to juice. Run chunks of watermelon through a blender or food processor, press it through a muslin cloth, jelly bag or fine sieve, and you've got plenty of watermelon juice. Is it still a Martini if you add watermelon juice? On a sunny summer day, who wants to argue the finer points of cocktails? It's time to fire up the barbecue.

- 50ml Sipsmith London Dry Gin
- 25ml dry vermouth
- 50ml fresh watermelon juice

Combine the ingredients in an ice-filled cocktail shaker. Shake. Strain into a chilled cocktail glass.

WINTER WARMERS

It's important to pay attention to temperature. Although we enjoy a number of chilled winter cocktails these days, that's a recent development. By the beginning of the 18th century, warm gin was sold by street vendors in steaming cups, especially popular during the 'Frost Fairs' on the Thames, when strikingly low temperatures froze the river solid. During those chilly years, Londoners ventured onto the ice in droves, and gin and gingerbread vendors followed.

Hot *Gin Twist*

During London's winter of 1822–3, the Thames was frozen by late December. Needless to say, hot drinks were all the rage, but none was hotter than a Gin Twist. Poet John Timb scribed 149 lines extolling its virtues. We revived it on a chilly day in the distillery and it has been an office favourite ever since. It was originally garnished with a lemon twist to prove the lemon juice was fresh and not from a bottle or barrel (even back then they knew fresh was far superior).

- 40ml Sipsmith London Dry Gin
- 25ml fresh lemon juice
- 25ml simple syrup (see page 26) or 1 heaped tablespoon sugar

To garnish: A large lemon twist

Bring a kettle of water to the boil. Combine the ingredients in a coffee mug. Add 100–150ml boiling water. Stir. Garnish with a large lemon twist.

Gin *Toddy*

Hot gin, lemon and honey or sugar. Such a simple drink, and one that has been around in various incarnations nearly as long as gin. A few centuries ago, people waxed lyrical about the welcoming ring of the toddy stick, a stirring stick used to mix this drink over countless tavern fires in pewter or copper vessels. The lemon was optional, a luxury for most. A splash of raspberry shrub might easily replace the imported citrus in rural establishments. Or perhaps no sour note at all, just the spirit, sugar or honey and boiling water.

- 50ml Sipsmith London Dry Gin
- 1 teaspoon honey
- 25ml fresh lemon juice or raspberry shrub

To garnish: A lemon wheel and a cinnamon stick

Bring a kettle of water to the boil. Combine the ingredients in a coffee mug. Add 100–150ml boiling water. Stir. Garnish with a lemon wheel and a cinnamon stick.

Essentially fruit infused in sweetened vinegar, shrubs are available in many shops, but are also remarkably easy to make. The internet is brimming with recipes, especially ones for raspberry shrub. Shrub is also growing in popularity as a mocktail, when combined with sparkling water.

Hot *Gin & Tonic*

While the Gin & Tonic traces back to the mid-1800s, the Hot Gin & Tonic is a drink we invented along with bartender Eoin Kenny at London's Ham Yard Hotel about four years ago. It was such an instant hit, you can now find this one around the world. The trick is the tonic syrup. Tonic water is actually nothing more than tonic syrup bottled with carbonated water. Tonic syrup is simple syrup flavoured with quinine (extracted from Cinchona bark), plus citrus and sometimes floral notes. Thankfully, these days there are quite a few tonic syrups available in the shops.

- 50ml Sipsmith London Dry Gin
- 25ml tonic syrup
- 150ml boiling water

To garnish: An orange twist

Combine the ingredients in a coffee mug or a heatproof rocks glass. Stir. Garnish with an orange twist.

FOOD PAIRING FAVOURITES

Mixed drinks have recently been rediscovered as competition to the predictable red, white or rosé on the dining table. Truth is, with some dishes a mixed drink is a far better pairing than wine. Try these as an interesting alternative at a dinner party or for a casual gathering of family, friends and food.

Bullshot

A drink that's as savoury and rich as beef tea? This is it. An unusual combination in the pantheon of classics, the Bullshot first became popular as a vodka-based drink, but has proven far better with gin. It can be served hot or cold and is most popular steaming from a thermos on a winter walk, accompanied by a sausage roll or a French dip sandwich. Delicious.

- 50ml Sipsmith London Dry Gin
- 100ml beef consommé (spiced to taste), hot or cold

For a cold serve: Combine the ingredients in an ice-filled rocks glass.

For a hot serve: Place the beef consommé in a microwaveable mug and heat until piping hot. Add the gin.

Reverse *Martini*

American celebrity chef Julia Child was a remarkable hostess and swore by this drink (not surprising, as she also said the two most important elements in the kitchen were steak and gin). She claimed this drink would pair better with fish than any white wine. We've tested this for years and she is still winning. Her mixing style was equally impressive. The first round was carefully measured: 3.5 parts dry vermouth to 1 part gin. The second was 2:1, then 1:1, then she put the gin bottle on the table and topped up drinks as needed.

- 15ml Sipsmith London Dry Gin
- 60ml dry vermouth
- 1 large lemon peel

Combine the ingredients in an ice-filled wine goblet or white wine glass. Stir.

Red *Snapper*

At its heart, this drink is simply a Bloody Mary made with gin. However, when you taste it, you'll agree that gin's herbaceous qualities and lack of sharpness compared to vodka make this a far superior combination, and the perfect drink to go with a big, greasy, fry up breakfast.

- 50ml Sipsmith London Dry Gin
- 150ml Bloody Mary mix
- Cracked black pepper

To garnish: A celery stick

Combine the gin and Bloody Mary mix in an ice-filled mixing glass. Let them rest together for 1 minute. Do not stir. Then, gently pour into an ice-filled highball glass. Sprinkle over a crack of black pepper and garnish with a celery stick.

Two-*Sherry*-*Tini*

This lovely Dry Martini variation was created, tested and retested at
The Halkin, London's first boutique hotel. Superb with fish; plaice and
sole especially.

- 50ml Sipsmith London Dry Gin
- 10ml Fino sherry
- 10ml Amontillado sherry

To garnish: A single olive

Combine the ingredients in an
ice-filled mixing glass. Stir. Strain into
a chilled cocktail glass. Garnish with
an olive.

Thyme *for Gin*

Thyme has bittersweet, aromatic flavours which pair perfectly with lemon. As Niki Segnit states in *The Flavour Thesaurus*, add juniper to the mix and you are on to a winner. Pair this with chicken or a Caesar salad.

- 50ml Sipsmith London Dry Gin
- 20ml thyme liqueur (we suggest Bigallet)
- 25ml fresh lemon sour mix (see page 26)

To garnish: A lemon wheel and 1 fresh thyme sprig

Combine the ingredients in an ice-filled cocktail shaker. Shake. Double strain into an ice-filled rocks glass or tumbler. Garnish with a lemon wheel and a sprig of fresh thyme.

CELEBRATORY SIPS

Is it wrong to mix with Champagne? It's certainly a sin to mix any ingredient with lesser ones. But use fresh juices, high-quality liqueurs and, of course, great gin and you simply end up with a celebration-worthy mix.

Gin *Spritz*

Spritzes boomed in the 1970s and '80s, then vanished except in outdoor cafés across Italy, where they had always been more mainstay than fad or fashion. Then, from Italy they rose again – this time with Campari or Aperol providing a refreshingly bitter theme. This drink cries out for a sunny afternoon, so much that it tastes like one whenever and wherever you try it.

🍸 20ml Sipsmith London Dry Gin
🍸 20ml Aperol
🍸 60ml Champagne

To garnish: An orange half wheel

Combine the gin and Aperol in an ice-filled wine glass. Top with Champagne. Garnish with an orange half wheel.

French 75

This drink is essentially a Tom Collins, but with Champagne instead of soda water. The ultimate, decadent aperitif, this combination of gin, lemon and Champagne has been around since at least 1915, when it first appeared at the New York Bar (now known as Harry's New York Bar) in Paris. The name was a salute to the French field artillery that would win the Great War for the Allies, perhaps because the drink has a similar kick to it.

🍹 25ml Sipsmith London Dry Gin
🍹 50ml fresh lemon sour mix (see page 26)
🍹 100ml Champagne

To garnish: A lemon twist

Combine the ingredients in a Champagne flute or coupe. Garnish with a lemon twist, or simply squeeze the twist over the drink and discard it, as any twist placed in a Champagne cocktail hastens the loss of bubbles.

Store the gin in the freezer before making this drink if you can. It is better for all the ingredients to go into the glass at the same serving temperature as the Champagne, just a few degrees above freezing.

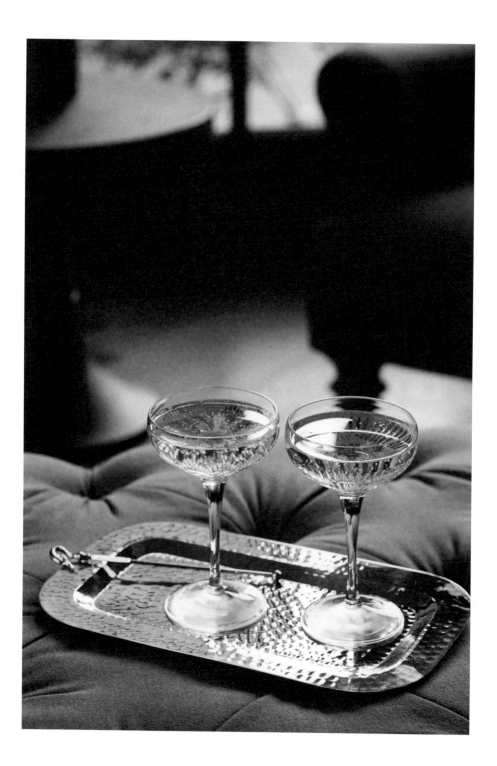

Millionaire's *Martini*

In the late 19th and early 20th centuries, Champagne taps were popular. You could screw one through the cork and get at the Champagne without opening the bottle. This way, you could also use a little at a time to top drinks. Champagne works well atop a surprising number of drinks – try a splash on the Bee's Knees (*see* page 57), Bramble (*see* page 99), or the Hanky Panky (*see* page 71). However, a personal favourite will always be the Martini. Try it on a night when you're opening Champagne anyway.

- 40ml Sipsmith London Dry Gin
- 10ml dry vermouth
- 40ml Champagne

To garnish: A lemon twist

Combine the gin and vermouth in an ice-filled mixing glass. Stir. Strain into a chilled cocktail glass. Squeeze a lemon twist over the drink and discard it. Top with Champagne.

Millionaire's *Mimosa*

Perfect for a boozy brunch or an early afternoon sipper, gin transforms the classic Mimosa into a properly balanced cocktail with herbaceous depth and dimension.

- 35ml Sipsmith London Dry Gin
- 50ml fresh orange juice
- 50ml Champagne

Combine the ingredients in a Champagne flute. It is even better if the gin has been chilled in the refrigerator or freezer.

PUDDING TIME

Drinks aficionados might sneer at sweet, creamy drinks, but more often than not it is because they try and, for obvious reasons, fail to pigeonhole them with aperitifs and cocktails. Think of these drinks as inspired replacements for Victoria sponge and blancmange. They can even be served in glasses on dessert plates, perhaps with a freshly baked biscuit on the side. We've done this at home many times.

Alexander

Sometimes there is no better pudding than a creamy pudding drink (for any Americans reading this: pudding means dessert, not literally pudding). The Brandy Alexander has had a lot more attention in recent years, but there is a reason it is called the 'Brandy' Alexander. This is because the Alexander was best-known with gin.

🍸 25ml Sipsmith London Dry Gin
🍸 25ml brown or white crème de cacao
🍸 25ml single cream

To garnish: Freshly grated nutmeg

Combine the ingredients in an ice-filled cocktail shaker. Shake well. Strain into a chilled cocktail glass. Garnish with a sprinkling of nutmeg.

Chiswick *in Black*

We recently discovered this drink in Japan, where a Tokyo bartender brought together three ingredients we never would have considered and made one of the best drinks we have tasted in ages. It has now become a team go-to in our distillery in Chiswick, especially after hours.

🥄 40ml Sipsmith London Dry Gin
🥄 20ml Kahlúa

To garnish: Cocoa powder

Wet half the rim of a chilled cocktail glass, then dip that half into the cocoa powder. Combine the gin and Kahlúa in an ice-filled mixing glass. Stir. Strain into the cocktail glass.

Gin *Milk Punch*

This may seem like one of the most bizarre drinks in the book, but that's the judgement of our modern palates and the flavour of our modern milk. Try this with full-fat local milk if you can get your hands on some and prepare to be pleasantly surprised. This is also a wonderful alternative to drinks modified with citrus or wines. (Note: If you're looking for a clarified milk punch, those recipes punch way beyond the simplicity of three ingredients.)

- 50ml Sipsmith London Dry Gin
- 100ml fresh full-fat milk
- 15–25ml simple syrup (see page 26)

To garnish: Freshly grated nutmeg

Combine the ingredients in an ice-filled rocks glass or tumbler. Transfer the contents to a cocktail shaker. Shake. Pour, unstrained – ice and all – back into the rocks glass or tumbler. Garnish with freshly grated nutmeg.

White *Cargo*

Gin and vanilla ice cream. It might sound like something new and awful, but this one actually comes from the legendary Harry Craddock of The Savoy Hotel, author of *The Savoy Cocktail Book*. And it is delicious. Look at the Ramos Gin Fizz: cream, egg, sugar, gin… Ice cream is practically a premix for a Ramos. The White Cargo was named after a play and silent film, starring Hedy Lamarr.

- 50ml Sipsmith London Dry Gin
- 50ml vanilla ice cream
- Splash of dry white wine

To garnish: Freshly grated nutmeg

Combine the ingredients in an empty cocktail shaker. Shake well without ice. Pour into a chilled cocktail glass. Garnish with a sprinkling of nutmeg.

Great *British Trifle*

This post-prandial, autumnal mix was created to resemble the flavour profile of a classic British pudding. It utilises our London Dry Gin, another British staple.

🌱 30ml Sipsmith London Dry Gin
🌱 20ml Byrrh Grand QuinQuina
🌱 10ml sherry (Pedro Ximenez is a Sipsmith team favourite)

To garnish: An orange twist

Combine the ingredients in an ice-filled cocktail shaker. Shake. Strain into a chilled cocktail glass. Garnish with an orange twist.

NIGHTCAPS

After the aperitif, after the cocktail hour, after dinner, the senses are sated and softened – and bold, bitter flavours are bound to appeal. Try some of these when the candles are burning low.

Gin & Aye

The blend of sherry, gin and whisky brings to mind the sipping of a martini next to a dwindling fire late at night. The rich and nutty notes from the sherry combined with the smokiness of the whisky are sure to send you off to sleep. Amontillado sherry works best in this drink.

* 30ml Sipsmith London Dry Gin
* 30ml sherry
* 10ml Islay whisky

Combine the ingredients in an ice-filled rocks glass. Stir.

Farmer's *Glory*

A powerful nightcap, sure to calm the nerves, this has long been used to cure just about any ailment. Originally made from just port and brandy, the addition of the most British of spirits boosted its popularity among the farmers who grew the ingredients for gin's base alcohol. A classic to mix at home, but not for the fainthearted.

- 🍸 10ml Sipsmith London Dry Gin
- 🍸 30ml brandy
- 🍸 30ml port

Mix the ingredients in a brandy glass. While most drinks are served cold or hot, this one is best a few degrees above room temperature. If you have one of those old brandy snifter warmers, which suspends a snifter over a candle and absolutely ruins a decent brandy, this is the one time you can make good use of it. Failing that, place the ingredients in a microwaveable mug instead, and heat until just warmed through.

Stout  Negroni

Stout makes an excellent mixer, especially when a couple of
the team from Fuller's Brewery drop off a mixed case of beer. This
drink was created several years ago, when a few of us (mainly Jared)
were mixing drinks in the distillery on a Friday night and had some
Fuller's Black Cab Stout on hand.

- 25ml Sipsmith London Dry Gin
- 25ml sweet vermouth
- 50ml stout

To garnish: A thin orange wedge

Combine the ingredients in an ice-filled rocks
glass. Stir. Garnish with a thin orange wedge.

Ginger Cat

This is an update on a little-known Sussex classic, loved by gin lovers. Usually topped with ginger wine, it is even better with a few dashes of Angostura bitters instead.

- 50ml Sipsmith London Dry Gin
- 100ml ginger ale
- 3–4 dashes of Angostura bitters

Combine the gin and ginger ale in an ice-filled highball glass. Top with dashes of Angostura bitters.

see overleaf >

Earl Grey *Sour*

This modern classic is a simplification of a drink created by our dear friend Audrey Saunders of Pegu Club in New York, around 2006. She worked out the perfect infusion of Earl Grey tea into gin – see below. This infused gin keeps for ages – not that it is likely to sit around once you taste it.

- 50ml Earl Grey-infused Sipsmith London Dry Gin*
- 25ml fresh lemon juice
- 20–25ml simple syrup (see page 26)

1 egg white (optional)

Combine the ingredients in an ice-filled cocktail shaker (add the egg white now if you are going to). Shake well. Strain into a chilled cocktail glass.

*Pour a bottle of gin into a jar or pitcher, add three Earl Grey tea bags and let it rest for an hour (don't leave it longer or it becomes too tannic). Remove the tea bags and your Earl Grey gin is ready to go. If you don't want a whole bottle of Earl Grey gin, you can infuse one-third of a bottle, about 250ml, with one tea bag for an hour.

see overleaf >

Sit & Stay

To sip with a sibling and debrief the shenanigans of a family dinner, or as a special tipple to toast the end of a great night with the last friends you don't want to leave – we simply love how the rosemary brings out the floral botanicals in our gin in this one.

- 50ml Sipsmith London Dry Gin
- 100ml fresh grapefruit juice
- 1 rosemary sprig

To garnish: Salt

Moisten the rim of a rocks glass with a little grapefruit juice and dip it into a saucer of salt, to coat the rim. Crack the rosemary sprig in three places, taking care not to break the stem (cracking it will 'wake up' the herb), and add it to the glass. Add ice, gin and then the grapefruit juice. Stir. Remove the rosemary once the potency is where you like it, as keeping it in the glass will allow the rosemary flavour to eventually overwhelm the drink.

NEW TAKES

There are a lot of drinks in this world, but there will always be more. A mathematician once calculated the possible combinations in a bar. His estimate was seventeen million. We haven't begun to scratch the surface, but with each generation of passionate mixers comes yet more additions to the lexicon – and we're proud to add the drinks in this chapter into the mix. Some may prove to be yesterday's news even before it's tomorrow. Others will stand beside or might even eclipse the known classics. Others are clearly steps in the evolution of the greats. All are simple to mix and are great opportunities to impress your dinner-party guests.

Gin *Penicillin*

Punch, the drinks industry magazine not its eponymous British predecessor, called this 'the most riffed-on modern classic'. Invented as a whisky drink by New York bartender Sam Ross in 2005, it is of course a riff itself, drawing influence from the Bee's Knees (*see* page 57) and its successors.

🍸 30ml Sipsmith London Dry Gin
🍸 20ml ginger wine
🍸 20ml fresh lemon juice

To garnish: A lemon half wheel

Combine the ingredients in an ice-filled cocktail shaker. Shake. Strain into an ice-filled rocks glass. Garnish with a lemon half wheel.

White *Negroni*

There are nearly as many ways to make a White Negroni as there are award-winning bartenders. However, the best was impossible until recent times because there was no clear substitute for Campari. Many bartenders tried Suze, a gentian liqueur, but it diverges from the Negroni with an earthy flavour. Try the new Luxardo Bitter Bianco. Close your eyes while tasting this drink and you will see red.

- 25ml Sipsmith London Dry Gin
- 25ml dry vermouth
- 25ml Luxardo Bitter Bianco

To garnish: An orange half-wheel or wedge

Combine the ingredients in an empty mixing glass. Pour into an ice-filled rocks glass or tumbler. There is no need to stir, just let it sit for a minute to soften as the ice melts. Garnish with an orange half-wheel or wedge.

London *Hi-Ball*

A twist on the classic London Calling, lengthened for a more refreshing and lighter beverage as recent drinking trends begin to favour lower-alcohol drinks and longer serves. It makes a refreshing after-dinner drink or all-day sipper.

- 40ml Sipsmith London Dry Gin
- 10ml Fino sherry
- Soda water, to top up

To garnish: A lemon wheel

Combine the gin and sherry in an ice-filled highball glass. Top with soda. Garnish with a lemon wheel.

Cucumber *Cups*

Canapés have been served in cucumber cups for ages. The cups are easy to make – you cut a cucumber into sections and scoop them out. These cups can then be chilled in the refrigerator and filled with a simple Martini to surprise your guests. We have served these as an amuse bouche-meets-aperitif. The following measures are per drink. Remember, the cucumber cups will not hold a standard-sized drink.

- 20ml Sipsmith London Dry Gin
- 20ml dry vermouth
- 1 cucumber cup

Combine the gin and vermouth in an ice-filled mixing glass. Stir. Strain into a cucumber cup.

Quite a few of the other drinks in this book would taste great served in a cucumber cup.

Modern *Pink Gin*

You can find the traditional recipe for Pink Gin on page 62. This version, which you still won't find to be a fruity, raspberry-hued drink, is balanced for modern palates. Funnily, the following recipe is the very definition of the cocktail – spirits, sugar, water and bitters – as it first appeared in 1806, so you could also call this a Gin Old Fashioned. The secret here is to add just enough sweetness to highlight the sweeter elements in the gin and bitters without making the drink itself perceptibly sweet.

- 50ml Sipsmith London Dry Gin
- 2–3 dashes of Angostura bitters
- 5ml simple syrup (see page 26)

To garnish: A raspberry

Combine the ingredients in an ice-filled mixing glass. Stir. Strain into a chilled cocktail glass. Garnish with a single raspberry.

Raspberry *Gin Sling*

While the Sling – spirits of any kind combined with sugar and water – pre-dates the cocktail, this Sling is brand new, dead simple and utterly moreish. One note of caution: you need to prepare the gin a week in advance. Don't give up now, it really is worth the bother. The result is a bright, blush-coloured cocktail that's definitely gin, but bursting with succulent raspberries.

- 50ml fresh raspberry Sipsmith London Dry Gin*
- 10ml simple syrup (see page 26)

To garnish: Fresh raspberries and an orange twist (optional)

Combine the gin and simple syrup in a mixing glass. Stir. Strain into a chilled cocktail glass. Garnish with fresh raspberries. You can also squeeze an orange twist over this drink, but discard it rather than setting it into the drink.

If you absolutely can't wait a week for the gin infusion, simply combine 50ml Sipsmith London Dry Gin and 4–5 frozen raspberries in a cocktail shaker, shake well and double strain. Use in place of the infused gin.

* Pour a bottle of Sipsmith London Dry Gin into a large Kilner or other clip-top jar. Add 250–300g fresh raspberries. Let it infuse for 7–10 days. Strain, discarding the raspberries, and re-bottle. You can also use this fresh raspberry-infused gin in a Gimlet (see page 78), a French 75 (see page 136) or virtually any other drink in this book if it strikes your fancy.

see overleaf >

Easy *Clover Club*

If you ever liked a Cosmopolitan cocktail, you have to love the Clover Club. In fact, it is quite similar to the original Cosmopolitan. It is said that the drink came from a members' club in Philadelphia around the late 1800s, and mentions in early 1900s newspapers tend to back that up. However, when the first recipe appeared in the *New York Herald* in 1909, it was a drink made with gin, fresh lemon juice, fresh lime juice, sugar and grenadine. Many other recipes emerged over the next decades. The Clover Club normally includes an egg white to make it creamy, but it's up to you.

- 50ml raspberry Sipsmith London Dry Gin (see opposite)
- 50ml fresh lemon sour mix (see page 26)
- 10ml grenadine (see page 187 for how to make your own)

An egg white (optional)

To garnish: Fresh raspberries

Combine the ingredients in an ice-filled cocktail shaker (add the egg white now if you are going to). Shake. Strain into a chilled cocktail glass. Garnish with raspberries.

see overleaf >

Gin *Twinkle*

Elderflowers are among the ubiquitous sights, scents and tastes of spring in the English countryside. Feel free to add more or less depending on how 'springy' you want this drink to be. If you're going to try making elderflower liqueur or cordial, remember to harvest the blossoms in the morning. That's when they have the most flavour. London bartender Tony Conigliaro created the original vodka version of this drink, but like most things in this world, the Twinkle is improved with gin.

- 25ml Sipsmith London Dry Gin
- 15–25ml elderflower liqueur or cordial
- 75ml English sparkling wine

To garnish: A small lemon twist

Combine the gin and elderflower liqueur in an ice-filled mixing glass. Stir. Strain into a Champagne flute or coupe. Top with sparkling wine. Garnish with a small lemon twist.

New Cross *Negroni*

Softer, sweeter and more approachable than the original, this version was born in London at MeatLiquor, where they use Carpano Antica vermouth, which is rich and balsamic.

- 25ml Sipsmith London Dry Gin
- 25ml Aperol
- 25ml sweet vermouth

To garnish: An orange wheel or wedge

Combine the ingredients in an ice-filled rocks glass or tumbler. Stir. Garnish with an orange wheel or wedge.

Holiday *Martini*

The Holiday Martini is a variation of the late-19th century Tuxedo Martini made famous by the Tuxedo Club near New York City. By using Fino sherry in the place of dry vermouth, the Holiday Martini balances the spice of the gin and the salty grape of the wine. The dryness of the two main components is tempered by the addition of Cocchi Americano, a sweet aromatised wine from northern Italy.

- 60ml Sipsmith London Dry Gin
- 20ml dry Fino sherry
- 5ml Cocchi Americano or Lillet Blanc

To garnish: A cocktail onion

Combine the ingredients in an ice-filled mixing glass. Stir. Strain into a Nick & Nora glass. Garnish with a cocktail onion.

The secret to mixing a good cocktail can be summed up in a single word: balance. When you are mixing a drink, you are seeking the perfect balance between strong and weak, and between savoury and sweet, and modifying these with a balance of spice. It is appropriate that the first time the word 'cocktail' was defined in print it was in a newspaper called *The Balance*. There, the drink was described as '...spirits of any kind, sugar, water and bitters...' This was a single-ingredient abbreviation of the classic punch formula, which had arrived in Europe with sailors returning from India in the late 16th century. (The ingredient that was lost in the move from punch to cocktail was citrus.)

Gin *Pom*

Fresh pomegranate juice only became widely available surprisingly recently. Twenty years ago, it was an exotic product. Now it is everywhere, and is a great mixer.

- 50ml Sipsmith London Dry Gin
- 50ml fresh pomegranate juice
- Soda water or sparkling wine, to top up

To garnish: A lemon half wheel and/or pomegranate seeds

Combine the ingredients in an ice-filled highball glass. Lift. Garnish with a lemon half wheel and/or pomegranate seeds.

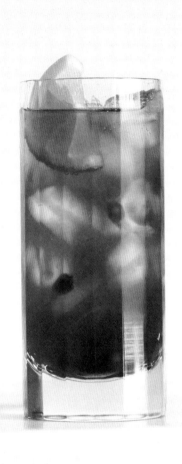

Lucky *Gin*

Named after Kingsley Amis' 1953 bestseller, *Lucky Jim*, this drink is adapted from one of the recipes in his 1972 book *On Drink*.

- 50ml Sipsmith London Dry Gin
- 5ml dry vermouth
- 10ml fresh cucumber juice

To garnish: A cucumber slice

Combine the ingredients in an ice-filled cocktail shaker. Shake. Strain into a chilled Martini glass. Garnish with a slice of cucumber.

If you don't have a juicer, grate a bit of cucumber and squeeze it with your hand over a bowl, then strain the collected juice.

Dark *Horse*

Based on a very old drink called the Stone Fence and born in a cocktail bar called The Dark Horse in Bath, UK, on a chilly afternoon, this combination of three ingredients works so well. It's an all-seasons drink, but especially good in autumn and winter.

- 25ml Sipsmith London Dry Gin
- 100ml dry cider
- 75ml ginger beer

Ice is optional in this drink. As long as the ingredients are chilled, you can simply combine them in a red wine or highball glass, or serve them over ice if you prefer.

Gin & (Apple) Juice

On our last trip Down Under it seemed like half the bars had a juicer going. We tried gin and freshly pressed apple juice. The juice was so fresh it was still foamy. Absolutely delicious! The second round was even better, as they dropped a thumb of fresh ginger into the juicer as well. We've been waiting for this to catch on in UK bars, but no luck yet. Thankfully, we have a juicer.

- 50ml Sipsmith London Dry Gin
- 100–150ml freshly pressed apple and ginger juice

To garnish: Apple slices and a fresh ginger slice (optional)

Combine the ingredients in an ice-filled highball glass. Stir. Garnish with apple slices and a slice of fresh ginger if you're feeling fancy.

Ginza *Collins*

This original long drink is creamy, citrusy and quenching. Calpis is a milk-based sweet drink and one of the top-selling soft drinks in Japan. Think of subtly lemony yogurt and you get an idea of the flavour. Outside Japan, it was renamed Calpico because the original name sounded like something else. It is sold as a syrup to be added to water or milk, but today also appears in nearly every Japanese vending machine with water or soda already added. If you can find Calpico (or Calpis) Soda, use that instead of the syrup and soda water listed below, to make the drink even easier to make.

- 25ml Sipsmith London Dry Gin
- 25ml Calpico syrup (Calpis syrup in Japan)
- 75ml soda water

To garnish: A lemon wheel

Combine the ingredients in an ice-filled highball glass. Lift. Garnish with a lemon wheel.

Atta *Boy*

This blush-coloured Martini twist is slightly more approachable than most and saw bursts of popularity in Australia in the 1950s and in the States in the 1970s, before it vanished. It is a drink we never would have considered recommending, except that there are now much better brands of grenadine – ones made from natural ingredients – available these days.

If a drink calls for grenadine, look for one that is made from pomegranates as the original stuff was. You can even make it at home during pomegranate season by combining the seeds of a pomegranate (don't worry about getting rid of all the white bits if you're peeling it) with 500ml water and 500g sugar. Simmer covered on low heat for 20 minutes. Set it aside to cool. Strain it and place it in a jar or bottle. Kept in the refrigerator, it will last at least a week.

- 40ml Sipsmith London Dry Gin
- 30ml dry vermouth
- 3-4 dashes of grenadine (or pomegranate molasses)

Combine the ingredients in an ice-filled mixing glass. Stir. Strain into a chilled cocktail glass.

G&P

Gin and pineapple seems like a strange combination, but it has actually been around for quite a while. Back in the 1930s there were even a few brands of pineapple-flavoured gin. Pineapple balances beautifully with Angostura bitters. You can use a lot of bitters if there's pineapple in the drink, as it takes the harsh edges off it, leaving the rich spices to come to the fore.

- 50ml Sipsmith London Dry Gin
- 100ml fresh pineapple juice
- 3–4 dashes of Angostura bitters

To garnish: A pineapple wedge

Combine the ingredients in an ice-filled cocktail shaker. Shake. Pour the contents, unstrained, ice and all, into a rocks glass or tumbler. Garnish with a pineapple wedge.

Gin *Tea*

One of our favourite cheats opens up a whole supermarket aisle of flavours for easy use in cocktails – the tea aisle. Pick any of the dozens of wonderful flavours available, such as red berry tea, or green tea with Japanese cherry, or ginger and strawberry green tea, to create your tea syrup. There are no limits with a good tea syrup. Once the syrup is made, you can even turn it into a liqueur simply by measuring how much you have and adding an equal quantity of gin to it. Then, you can bottle it up for later.

- 50ml Sipsmith London Dry Gin
- 25ml fresh lemon juice
- 25ml homemade tea syrup*

Combine the ingredients in an ice-filled cocktail shaker. Shake. Strain into a chilled cocktail glass.

Alternatively, combine the ingredients in an ice-filled rocks glass and stir. Or, combine in an ice-filled highball glass and top with soda.

*Heat 500ml water with 500g sugar on a low heat, stirring until the sugar dissolves, then bring it up to a simmer. Add a few tea bags and set it aside to cool. Lift out the tea bags after about ten minutes and you have a simple and delicious-flavoured syrup, as well as a seemingly endless palette for making more.

Swan *Collins*

The Swan Collins is a delicate, floral twist on the classic Tom Collins cocktail. It works equally well with our Lemon Drizzle Gin for a lemon-sherbet finish to the drink.

- 35ml rose-infused Sipsmith London Dry Gin*
- 50ml fresh lemon sour mix (see page 26)
- 100ml soda water

To garnish: A lemon half wheel and edible rose petals

Combine the ingredients in an ice-filled highball glass. Lift. Garnish with a lemon half wheel and edible rose petals.

*Pour a bottle of Sipsmith London Dry Gin into a large Kilner or other clip-top jar. Add the petals from a couple of edible roses and leave to infuse for up to 48 hours, then strain. If you go for red or pink roses they will add a lovely colour to the gin, which in turn will give the drink a beautiful pink hue. Alternatively, you can add 30 drops of good-quality rose essence (not rose water) to a bottle of Sipsmith London Dry Gin and shake well to mix.

Green-Eyed *Swan*

The Green-Eyed Monster features equal parts Green Chartreuse, gin and sweet vermouth. By swapping the sweet vermouth for pineapple juice you have a fresh, fruity twist on this aromatic drink.

↗ 35ml Sipsmith London Dry Gin
↗ 35ml Green Chartreuse
↗ 35ml fresh pineapple juice

To garnish: 1 pineapple leaf

Combine the ingredients in an ice-filled cocktail shaker. Shake. Double strain into a chilled cocktail glass. Garnish with a pineapple leaf.

Marksmith

A favourite drink of ours for ages, it finally got a name when a dear friend of Sipsmith, Pryce Greenow, visited the distillery on a Friday afternoon (an excellent time for friends to visit). After a few, he proclaimed this combination of Sipsmith and Maker's Mark delicious and dubbed it the Marksmith.

- 25ml Sipsmith London Dry Gin
- 25ml Maker's Mark Whisky
- 25ml sweet vermouth

To garnish: A cocktail cherry or an orange twist

Combine the ingredients in an ice-filled mixing glass. Stir. Alternatively, this is a great drink to throw (see page 23). Strain into a chilled cocktail glass. Garnish with a cocktail cherry or an orange twist.

Office *Martini*

It is hard to say when and where our infatuation with dry sherry began
(everyone around the table glances at Sam with a smile), but there's no
question that it makes a glorious Martini. Many a distillery Friday
afternoon was toasted away with a round of these. Thus the name.

- 50ml Sipsmith London Dry Gin
- 25ml Fino sherry
- 1 dash of orange bitters (very optional)

To garnish: A lemon twist

Combine the ingredients in an ice-filled
mixing glass. Stir. Strain into a chilled
cocktail glass. Garnish with a lemon twist.

Cherry *Bomb*

This playful drink is all about the fun. Add some popping candy to the tip of your tongue and take a sip. The crackle and pop from the popping candy gradually dissipates to leave citrus, cherry and juniper.

- 35ml Sipsmith London Dry Gin
- 15ml Heering Cherry Liqueur
- 25ml fresh lemon sour mix (see page 26)

To garnish: A sachet of popping candy

Combine the ingredients in an ice-filled cocktail shaker. Shake. Double strain into a chilled cocktail glass. Garnish with a sachet of popping candy on the side.

Cranberry *Sip*

Fresh cranberries are so much better than cranberry juice, which usually contains less than 25 per cent cranberry juice. They are also easy to use if you have a muddler or a rolling pin.

- 50ml Sipsmith London Dry Gin
- 10–12 fresh cranberries
- 15ml simple syrup (see page 26)

To garnish: A lime wheel or 1 fresh cranberry

Thoroughly muddle the cranberries in a cocktail shaker (see page 113). Add the gin, simple syrup and ice. Shake well. Double strain into a chilled cocktail glass. Garnish with a lime wheel or a cranberry.

Gin *Caipirinha*

The national drink of Brazil can be a refreshing yet potent beverage. The name translates roughly to 'Little Country Girl' and it is made with cachaça, fresh lime pieces and sugar. This gin version balances the citric nature of the lime with the floral aspect of the honey.

- 50ml Sipsmith London Dry Gin
- ½ lime, cut into quarters
- 2 tablespoons honey

Combine the lime wedges and honey in an empty rocks glass. Muddle to release the juices (see page 113). Fill the glass with ice and add the gin. Transfer the contents into a cocktail shaker and shake vigorously. Dump back into the original rocks glass.

Optional: Substitute Sipsmith Sloe Gin for London Dry and cut the honey by half.

Gin *Faux-Jito*

San Francisco is a hot bed for Tiki culture and, not being connoisseurs of rum cocktails, when the Sipsmith Team visited our friends across the pond, we ended up asking for a simple gin cocktail with a refreshing twist – this has been a go-to drink ever since.

- 50ml Sipsmith London Dry Gin
- 25ml fresh lime sour mix (see page 26)
- 100ml soda water

To garnish: Mint sprigs

Combine the ingredients in an ice-filled collins glass. Lift. Garnish with a bunch of mint sprigs.

Dark *Fruit Bramble*

The Bramble is a gin cocktail which needs no introduction. This version builds on the classic (*see* page 99) with a Sipsmithian twist.

- 50ml Sipsmith London Dry Gin
- 25ml fresh lemon juice
- 3 tablespoons blackberry or blackcurrant jam

To garnish: A lemon twist and dark fruits (blackberries, blackcurrants, mulberries or blueberries)

Combine the ingredients in an ice-filled cocktail shaker. Shake well. Strain into a rocks glass or tumbler filled with crushed ice or cubes. Garnish with dark fruits and a lemon twist.

Gin *Paloma*

The origin of the Paloma is broadly debated as no one is certain who created it. Many believe that the legendary Don Javier Delgado Corona, owner of La Capilla bar in the town of Tequila, Mexico, may have been responsible for its creation. One of his famous drinks included Tequila, Coca-Cola and lime juice. The Paloma originally consisted of Tequila, lime and grapefruit soda, but this version of course includes gin, which partners perfectly with all of the citrus flavours in the original recipe.

- 50ml Sipsmith London Dry Gin
- 10ml fresh lime juice
- 100–150ml fresh pink grapefruit juice

To garnish: Salt and a grapefruit twist

Moisten the rim of a rocks glass or tumbler with a little grapefruit juice and dip it into a saucer of salt, to coat the rim. Fill the glass with ice and add the ingredients. Lift to combine. Garnish with a grapefruit twist.

Gin *Espresso Martini*

While the Espresso Martini is one of the more popular vodka drinks today, it is actually better with gin. It is also very simple to make if you know the secret. The difference between a great one and a weak attempt can be spotted from across the room. Look for the 'crema', as barristas call the foam on top of a good espresso, built by shaking the drink a little harder than other drinks, but just a little.

- 50ml Sipsmith London Dry Gin
- 25ml espresso
- 25ml coffee liqueur, triple sec or simple syrup (see page 26)

To garnish: 3 coffee beans or an orange twist

Combine the ingredients in an ice-filled cocktail shaker. Shake very well. Strain into a chilled cocktail glass. Garnish with coffee beans or an orange twist.

Lords *G&T*

While playing with drinks for Lords, the home of cricket, we came across this wonderful twist on the classic G&T. No doubt W G Grace would have been happy to knock a few of these down before knocking a few out of the ground.

- 🥄 50ml Sipsmith London Dry Gin
- 🥄 15ml port
- 🥄 7.5ml tonic water

To garnish: A plum fan

Combine the ingredients in an ice-filled highball glass. Lift. Garnish with a plum fan.

To make a plum fan, slice a plum in half lengthwise. Remove the stone and place one half cut side down on a chopping board. Make thin, even slices lengthwise (five or six should do), and then fan them out on top of the drink.

Limoncello *Collins*

Limoncello is surprisingly under-utilised as a mixer in cocktails. While many classics call for triple sec or Cointreau, this national liqueur of Italy (much as sloe gin could be considered the national liqueur of Britain) was overlooked. However, it is every bit as good a mixer. It is also easy to make. If you're feeling adventurous, there are lots of good recipes online.

- 25ml Sipsmith London Dry Gin
- 25ml limoncello
- Soda water, to top up

To garnish: A lemon twist

Combine the gin and limoncello in an ice-filled highball glass. Top with soda water. Lift. Garnish with a lemon twist.

SLOE IT DOWN

So there you have it, 100 delicious cocktail recipes showcasing every facet of the wonderful drink that is gin, as promised on the front of this book. But wait… just when you think the last drop has been finished, there's more! We couldn't write this book without a nod to sloe gin, a whole separate category of taste, but made with the same great gin that you've used so far.

Over the coming pages, we'll explain just what sloe gin is, how to make it (honestly, it's easy) and a handful of cocktails you can make with it. Think of this as rather like the bonus tracks on an album – an unexpected treat. And if you don't fancy making sloe gin at home, we have made our very own fabulous Sipsmith Sloe Gin, which you can always use instead.

HOW TO MAKE
SLOE GIN

Sloe gin is to Britain what limoncello is to Italy. Everyone makes it and everyone is proud of their efforts and likely to offer it after supper whenever there are guests at the table. Trouble is, the British recipe is rather terrible, and for generations the best sloe gins were made through desperate efforts to compensate for its shortcomings.

Sloe gin only came into being because, when large country properties were divided into smallholdings in the early and mid-Victorian era, farmers found the dense and thorny blackthorn tree to be a good hedging plant. Suddenly, the countryside was rife with tiny, bitter, blue-black plums. They were unpalatable, but British farmers were resourceful. They tried for a decade to make sloe wine. Even parsnip wine is better than sloe wine (yes, we did a comparison test), so that fell by the wayside.

Then, a sloe gin recipe emerged, instructing people to harvest the fruit after the first frost and under a full moon, then to prick each with a silver pin (full moon, silver pin... did they think these were werewolves or something?). Next, you combine the sloes with gin and sugar. You shake the jar once a week or so until Christmas, in part to get the sugar to dissolve. Innumerable later recipes added that you could use cheap gin as it is 'just an ingredient'. And this recipe is still in use today. Face, meet palm.

Making far-better sloe gin is actually easier than this. Pick sloes when they are ripe. You can't taste them to check, but it is still easy to tell. When ripe, they feel like tiny ripe plums, and develop a powdery coating of airborne yeast.

We tried pricking them, but only to say we had done it. Instead we handled them the way we treat most fruit that we want to infuse into spirit – we put it in the freezer for a couple of days. This ruptures the fruit flesh like a thousand pins, and is a much better option.

Next, combine the gin and fruit. Fill a large Kilner or clip-top jar a third or half full with sloes, and then fill with gin. There is no fermentation or other alchemy that requires sugar here. In fact, sugar saturates the spirit, creating an osmotic pressure barrier which prevents the spirit from extracting the natural fruit sugars.

And cheap gin? We've never seen a Sunday roast recipe that said 'use cheap beef, it's just an ingredient'. Early on we made ten sloe gins, identical except for the gin, and let our neighbours taste them. They unanimously selected the ones made with good gin. Ingredients matter!

Now the gin and sloes need to rest for a minimum of two months and, importantly, for a maximum of five months. Think of the flavour as a bell curve. It hits a peak in two or three months. By six months it develops an underlying flavour like you found an old sponge under the sink and added that. At the two-year mark, it takes on another undertone, as if you ran over oak leaves in a muddy puddle with a Land Rover a few times and then added a measure of that.

When you take the gin off the fruit, this is the time to sweeten it – and, because you've waited for this step, you get to sweeten it to taste rather than hoping you've got the sugar balanced from the start. Use simple syrup (see page 26) and add a little at a time, tasting as you go. There are worse ways to spend an afternoon.

Now, by harvesting when the sloes are ripe, freezing them for a couple of days, adding the sugar at the end – and, most importantly, by using good gin – you can make the best possible sloe gin.

We weren't sure how it would be received when we said, 'Sloe gin? Britain, you're doing it wrong!' As one does with a secret formula, we put it in *The Times*, the *Telegraph* and a couple of other papers, and went on TV (on Alan Titchmarsh's show, to be precise) to give it away there as well. *The Times* was the first to reply, saying it was simply 'Britain's best sloe gin.'

Winter *Gin & Tonic*

Another Sipsmith original, this Gin & Tonic with just a little sloe gin heralds the arrival of sloe gin around the festive season. Sloe gin on its own is a bit heavy with tonic, but we found – after extensive experimentation – the combination of gin and sloe gin is delicious.

- 25ml Sipsmith London Dry Gin
- 15ml Sipsmith Sloe Gin
- 100–150ml tonic

Combine the ingredients in an ice-filled highball glass. Lift. Garnish with an orange wedge.

To garnish: An orange wedge

Charlie *Chaplin*

Supposedly the silent screen star's favourite drink in pre-Prohibition New York, the Charlie Chaplin first appeared in a post-Repeal book written by Oscar of the Waldorf in 1934. The combination of sloe gin and apricot brandy might appear to be overly sweet, but the fresh lime juice balances the drink.

- 25ml Sipsmith Sloe Gin
- 25ml apricot brandy
- 25ml fresh lime juice

Combine the ingredients in an ice-filled cocktail shaker. Shake well. Strain into a chilled cocktail glass.

We found this drink also worked really well with 2 parts London Dry Gin to 1 part each of the other ingredients. The measures are easier if you mix 2 drinks at once: 50ml Sipsmith London Dry Gin, 25ml Sipsmith Sloe Gin, 25ml apricot brandy and 25ml fresh lime juice.

Sloe & Lemon

This lighter, softer version of the Gin & Lemon combines sloe gin (which is lower in strength than London Dry) with lemon tonic, which balances the sweetness of the sloe gin. We can promise you, we have tested this extensively in the distillery.

- 50ml Sipsmith Sloe Gin
- 100–150ml lemon tonic water
- 1 orange wedge

To garnish: An orange wheel

Combine the sloe gin and lemon tonic in an ice-filled highball glass. Squeeze the orange wedge into the drink and discard it. Lift to mix. Garnish the drink with the orange wheel.

Hot Mulled Sloe

For a warming festive toast which beats the trousers off mulled wine, Mulled Sloe ticks the box. Mulled wine seems like such a good idea, but invariably becomes a bit of a letdown as tannic solids from the wine accumulate on your tonsils. Hot wine is really only good in Bolognese sauce or coq au vin. Sloe gin, on the other hand, truly shines as a warm drink. This one was invented in the Sipsmith distillery.

- 50ml Sipsmith Sloe Gin
- 1 sachet of mulling spices
- 100ml cloudy apple juice

Combine the spices and apple juice in a microwaveable mug. Heat on high for 1 minute or as long as it takes to start steaming. Let it rest for a few minutes, then remove the spices. Add the sloe gin.

INDEX